"There is a great need today to get behind the Reformers and rediscover the sources of their theology and piety. The substance of the great fathers of the church will propel evangelicals into a deeper level of theological thought and ecumenical dialogue. *Evangelicals and Tradition* will initiate that discussion and lead the way."

Robert Webber, Myers Professor of Ministry, Northern Seminary

"In response to the pressures of modern culture, the church has dulled its message. But that message can regain its edge if evangelicals will listen to the demands of the gospel through the ears of the church fathers. *Tradition* used to be a 'fightin' word' for Protestants, but Williams argues that, with the proper approach, tradition can be evangelicals' ally instead of their enemy."

David Neff, editor and vice president, Christianity Today

"Evangelicalism is best defined as a renewal movement within historic Christian orthodoxy. This volume explores a major wellspring of that renewal—the evangelical appropriation of Christian tradition. It is an important contribution to theological *ressourcement*."

Timothy George, dean, Beeson Divinity School;
executive editor, *Christianity Today*

"The Protestant Reformation began as a call for the church catholic to receive the evangelical word of Scripture. Over time, evangelical Christianity lost its sense of catholicity. Williams has emerged as one of the leading voices of this generation calling for the retrieval of the evangelical catholic heritage of the Reformation. More importantly, he shows how to integrate the retrieved tradition into the theological reflections of contemporary evangelicalism. This book deserves to be widely read and wisely practiced."

Curtis W. Freeman, research professor of theology and director,
Baptist House of Studies, Duke Divinity School

"Williams has brought a new sense of engagement to the ancient task of relating Scripture, tradition, and spiritual experience. Evangelicals need to be reminded that there is a truly catholic tradition that goes back to the apostles that belongs to them as much as it does to other Christians. This book roots us in the living faith of every age and should be welcomed by everyone who wants to grow in the knowledge and love of Christ."

Gerald Bray, Anglican professor of divinity, Beeson Divinity School,
Samford University

EVANGELICAL *RESSOURCEMENT*
ANCIENT SOURCES FOR THE CHURCH'S FUTURE

D. H. Williams, series editor

The Evangelical *Ressourcement:* Ancient Sources for the Church's Future series is designed to address the ways in which Christians may draw upon the thought and life of the early church to respond to the challenges facing today's church.

EVANGELICALS
AND TRADITION

The Formative
Influence of the
Early Church

D. H. WILLIAMS

B)
Baker Academic
Grand Rapids, Michigan

Published by Baker Academic
a division of Baker Publishing Group
P.O. Box 6287, Grand Rapids, MI 49516-6287
www.bakeracademic.com

Printed in the United States of America

Library of Congress Cataloging-in-Publication Data
Williams, Daniel H.
    Evangelicals and tradition : the formative influence of the early church / D. H. Williams.
        p.   cm. — (Evangelical ressourcement)
    Includes bibliographical references and index.
    ISBN 0-8010-2713-6 (pbk.)
    1. Evangelicalism. 2. Tradition (Theology) 3. Fathers of the church. I. Title
II. Series.
BR1640.W54 2005
230'.044—dc22   2004024241

To Cindy, Ryan, and Chad,
who came with me to a different country
and together journey still

CONTENTS

SERIES PREFACE

THE EVANGELICAL RESSOURCEMENT: Ancient Sources for the Church's Future series is designed to address the ways in which Christians may draw upon the thought and life of the early church to respond to the challenges facing today's church. The term *ressourcement* was coined by French Roman Catholic writers in the mid-twentieth century as descriptive of theological renewal that declared Christians must return to the sources (*ad fontes*) of the ancient Christian tradition. The operative assumption was that the church is apostolic (formed and directed by the Old and New Testaments) and also patristic (indebted to the intellectual and spiritual legacy of the fathers of the church). Much of our understanding of the Bible and theological orthodoxy, directly or indirectly, has come through the interpretive portals of the early church, which is an integral part of the Protestant identity, no less than it is for Roman Catholicism or Eastern Orthodoxy.

Using the methods and tools of patristic scholarship, each series volume is devoted to a particular theme related to biblical and theological interpretation. Similar to the past practices of *ressourcement*, this series is not seeking to appropriate the contributions of the early church in an idealized sense but through a critical utilization of the fathers as the church's primary witnesses and architects for faithfully explicating the Christian faith. Series readers will see how (1) Scripture and the early tradition were both necessary for the process of orthodox teaching, (2) there is a reciprocal relationship between theology and the life of the church, (3) the liberty of the Spirit in a believer's life must be balanced with the continuity of the church in history, and (4) the Protestant Reformation must be integrated within the larger and older picture of what it means to be catholic. In effect, it is the intention of this series to reveal how historical Protestantism was inspired and shaped by the patristic church.

As Protestantism confronts the postdenominational and, in many ways, post-Christian world of the twenty-first century, it is vital that its future identity not be constructed apart from the fullness of its historical foundations. Seminal to these foundations is the inheritance of the early church, "that true, genuine Christianity, directing us to the strongest evidence of the Christian doctrine" (John Wesley). Therein Christians will find not a loss of their distinctiveness as Protestants but, as the sixteenth-century Reformers found, the resources necessary for presenting a uniquely Christian vision of the world and its message of redemption.

PREFACE

AFTER READING THE reviews of a previously published book,[1] you develop a sense of which of your arguments
were insightful and useful, which were probably wrong and need
correction, and which ones you said too little about. Each of the
three kinds of criticism are useful, but the most challenging of
the three is the latter one because it reveals gaps and unfulfilled
parts of your argument. For many of these insights I am grateful,
and I have had the sense from nearly every reviewer that we are
together engaged in a task of reenvisioning Protestantism that is
not and must not be restricted by the anti-Catholic polemics of
the sixteenth and seventeenth centuries (and that are still perpetu-
ated today). It is time to move on.

My learned friend Peter Erb at Wilfrid Laurier University commented on the historical character of my book with the troubling
words, "At the root of his book, however, Williams cannot avoid
the challenge as posited by Cardinal Newman's adage, 'To be deep
in history is to cease to be a Protestant.'"[2] Erb should know that
he laid down the gauntlet with this remark, for in the end (though
not the end of this particular book), I hope I am able to prove

1. D. H. Williams, *Retrieving the Tradition and Renewing Evangelicalism: A Primer for
Suspicious Protestants* (Grand Rapids: Eerdmans, 1999).
2. Peter Erb, *Conrad Grebel Review* 19, no. 2 (Spring 2001): 109.

Newman wrong by showing that the necessity of appropriating doctrinal history in the preservation of Christian orthodoxy is no less true for the Protestant free church than it is for any other species of Protestantism. To be "deep in history" for evangelical Protestantism need not be and should not be oxymoronic. One should not have to leave evangelicalism or a believers' church setting to be nourished by the substantial resources available in ancient (or patristic) Christianity. The great model for this undertaking was and is Philip Schaff, whose scholarly work of the last century in producing translations of the primary texts of church history, the early church especially, is a sufficient demonstration that any oxymoron between Protestantism and the whole of the church's history is artificially self-imposed. It is not necessarily built into the original fabric of the Protestant spirituality. This can be welcome news to many believers who wonder about the seemingly empty content and ahistoricalism of their worship services. To redress the balance, this book presents evidence that is drawn from historical and theological resources. It may bring unaccustomed exercise to some, but I hope not frustration. Frankly, the only way to discover the wellspring of patristic resources is to present them in all their diversity and uniqueness.

Another challenge posed by my interlocutors on the subject of tradition has to do with how I halt more or less at the fifth century when it comes to identifying the church's tradition. Like the nineteenth-century Oxford tractarians, my development of tradition was confined to the early church. Surely tradition continued after the Council of Chalcedon (451), a point I acknowledge but did not stress. At the time I was writing *Retrieving the Tradition* in 1998, it seemed like enough of an accomplishment to convince my free church and evangelical readers that there *was* a tradition that originally functioned cooperatively with scriptural testimony and that this tradition carried an authority that was necessary for defining the true or catholic faith. Nevertheless, the criticism is a valid one and deserves to be answered by facing the implications of the tradition as a canon of faith.

Overall, the reception of my theses articulated in earlier books and articles demonstrates that a deep hunger exists among various communions of Protestants for the rediscovery of the church's historical witness as mediated by Scripture and tradition. Such rediscovery, of course, includes the way in which the Christian past impacts present worship and spirituality. This is not a project merely about reinvigorating interest in the early church. But whether the efforts at retrieving the historical cornerstones of the early church will result or even could result in spiritual and ecclesiastical renewal[3] remains to be seen. Certainly, these efforts will not be sufficient unless they are directed by the Spirit of God, who "searches all things, even the deep things of God" (1 Cor. 2:10). What the forms of "renewal" ought to look like once they happen is a debatable point and will continue to be so. At the very least, however, the degree of understanding that continues to grow between evangelicals and Roman Catholics on the essentials of the Christian faith is an encouraging sign of renewal in the church of Christ. The last decade or so of ecumenical dialogues and publications issued between evangelical groups and Roman Catholic representatives have been fruitful for creating greater mutuality (not denominational unity and certainly not doctrinal uniformity) on basic doctrines and practices. The conversations going on with Evangelicals and Catholics Together,[4] the international dialogues on pertinent theological matters between Roman Catholics and Protestants sponsored by the World Evangelical Association,[5] and the unnumbered pastoral and lay study groups seeking a deeper understanding of their faith in light of the broader picture of the faith are positive developments that bode well for the church's future. There is, moreover, a new openness on the part of free church Protestants to hear and incorporate the contributions of Eastern Orthodoxy into the theological conversation.

Implicit to the agenda in the pages that follow is how Christian tradition retains its formative character through time and undergoes change. Given the dynamic nature of tradition as a living activity and process, rather like a spoken language, it cannot be immune to alteration and development. There is always the creation of new syntheses and emphases that may introduce

3. A question raised in Everett Ferguson, "Article Review," *Scottish Journal of Theology* 55 (2002): 101.

4. Charles Colson and Richard John Neuhaus, eds., *Your Word Is Truth: A Project of Evangelicals and Catholics Together* (Grand Rapids: Eerdmans, 2002).

5. Formerly the World Evangelical Fellowship. See the Vatican's summary of this committee's progress report, *The Pontifical Council for Promoting Christian Unity* 106 (2001): 29–30.

significant modification. But no less a reality is the durable character of tradition,[6] which preserves and defines the fundamentals of Christian belief. This character of tradition does not exist in an abstract form or ideal place. How change occurs within the tradition has created a mighty host of issues among Roman Catholics and Protestants. These are matters that deserve the Christian believer's time and effort. They are neither purely academic nor intellectual fodder for sustaining the ecumenical agenda. At stake here is what doctrinal faithfulness looks like and how it was initially defined, a critical issue for Christian churches in our post-Christian and postfoundational culture.

Finally, I should comment on my use of "Roman Catholic" instead of "Catholic" as the preferred designation for my fellow pilgrims. I remain steadfast on the point, made numerous times before, that the catholicism of the earliest Christian centuries is not the same thing as the religious communion known as Roman Catholicism. It can rightly be argued that there are roots in the latter traceable to the former. Customarily, Catholic (capital C) is used as a shorthand for Roman Catholic, but to say that Roman Catholicism is the sole and inevitable development of catholicism is not tenable. No one communion can represent itself as a privileged extension of the early church. The use of the epithet "catholic" is not uniquely of Rome. They are indeed catholic, but so are Protestants and Eastern Orthodox. The confession of the Apostles' Creed in "one, holy, and catholic church" is for every believer to declare and believe.

Let me express my thanks to Robert Hosack, senior editor of Baker Academic, who provided the initial stimulus for this volume and for the series of which this book is the first installment. No less of my appreciation goes to Prof. Fred Norris, who kindly read and offered valuable criticism on early drafts. I am grateful for the mix of friendship, ministry, and academic professionalism we share. Jeffrey Cary, my graduate assistant at Baylor University, also read chapters and helped bring clarity to parts of my arguments. Given the overall quality of assistance received, I hope that I have been able to translate it into writing.

DHW

6. See Robert Wilken, "The Durability of Orthodoxy," *Word and World* 8 (1988): 124–32.

INTRODUCTION

> We agreed that if we could start seminary again we would devote
> more time to church history and patristics. Alas! Those are areas
> many people begin to appreciate only as they mature and accu-
> mulate experience.
>
> B. J. Bailey and J. M. Bailey,
> *Who Are the Christians in the Middle East?*

A NERVE WITHIN CONTEMPORARY evangelical-
ism has been hit, and its effects are ushering in enormous
potential change. Discussion of the place and value of the great
tradition is taking place among pastors and laity in denominations
that have normally regarded it as irrelevant or as a hindrance to
authentic Christian belief and spirituality. This new openness to
hearing the tradition represents an extraordinary work of the Spirit
in our time. The last half decade or so has seen a readiness among
evangelicals and many mainline Protestants to open the door that
has been closed to tradition, finding in it potential resources for
understanding their own Christian heritage. Likewise, a literature
is beginning to develop around the notion of Christian tradition,
especially as it concerns the relevance of the legacy of the early
church for today's church.[1]

1. J. Cutsinger, ed., *Reclaiming the Great Tradition* (Downers Grove, Ill.: InterVarsity,
1997); Robert Webber, *Ancient-Future Faith* (Grand Rapids: Baker, 1999); D. H. Williams,

During the centuries following the Roman Catholic Council of Trent (1545–63), many Protestants regarded the concept of tradition as the radically "other," a kind of competing authority to biblical authority. Even for most of the twentieth century, tradition was associated with the practices of Roman Catholicism,[2] which had a decidedly negative connotation. Inherent to evangelical and free church circles is an anticredal perspective, which has played a key role in theological outlook and interpretation of the Bible. Creeds have been commonly regarded as a kiss of death, either as violations of one's spiritual liberty or as stiff and deadening forms of Christian expression.

The Council of Trent's two-source theory of revelation, written and unwritten, seemed to Protestant critics clear evidence of Roman reliance on two separate sources of revelation, Scripture and tradition, and that these were two equivalent authorities. It is remarkable that the mandate of receiving the church's whole tradition, both written and unwritten, legislated in the seventh ecumenical Council of Nicaea (787)—which various Protestant communions accept as authoritative[3]—has been completely ignored by anti-Catholic apologists. Nevertheless, inclusion of tradition demonstrated to Protestants that Roman Catholicism had betrayed the primacy of scriptural authority. Despite the fact that other voices among their ranks have warned against such a facile position, the Bible has been and continues to be used as if it were an antidote to most of Christian history. The longstanding principles of *sola scriptura* (Scripture alone) and the priesthood of every believer, especially as it pertains to a personal understanding of the Bible, have served to isolate Scripture from its place within the church's history. More than one sincere Christian believer or pastor has turned the divine character of Scripture into the antithesis to everything else historical in the church. With good intentions, but oblivious to the damage they are causing to Chris-

---

Retrieving the Tradition and Renewing Evangelicalism: A Primer for Suspicious Protestants (Grand Rapids: Eerdmans, 1999); Charles Colson and Richard John Neuhaus, eds., *Your Word Is Truth: A Project of Evangelicals and Catholics Together* (Grand Rapids: Eerdmans, 2002); and Stephen Holmes, *Listening to the Past: The Place of Tradition in Theology* (Grand Rapids: Baker Academic, 2002).

2. See John Woodbridge, "The Role of 'Tradition' in the Life and Thought of Twentieth-Century Evangelicals," in *Your Word Is Truth*, 103–46.

3. See chap. 2 below.

tian perception of its own legacy, some evangelical and free church leaders, in their desire to safeguard the distinctives of Protestant orthodoxy, have decried the very heart of the Christian faith.

Far worse than suspicion or opposition, however, is ignorance. A multitude of leaders within the free church tradition (Baptist, Christian Church/Disciples of Christ, Church of Christ, Church of God, Nazarene, Evangelical Free, Bible churches, Christian and Missionary Alliance, Mennonite, etc.) rarely bother with questions about the role of the church's ancient tradition or its relation to Scripture. On the one hand, the contemporary crush of being ecclesial administrators, family therapists, and persuasive marketers for their congregations' programs absorbs most of their energy. As important as theological debates over the nature of authority may be, they are, quite simply, immaterial to the tasks at hand. (Since this is my own faith context, I do not idly write these words.) The fact that Protestant congregations expect good sermons from their pastors has little to do, unfortunately, with solid theological content based on using the best of the church's intellectual and spiritual resources. A growing number of these same pastors are rightly dissatisfied with their designated role of "keepers of the institution." They recognize, in accord with the exhortation given to Timothy, "guard what has been entrusted to your care" (1 Tim. 6:20), that the pastoral role consists of preserving and transmitting the Christian faith.

On the other hand, the theological ignorance of the church's tradition reflects the way in which many clergy and Christian leaders have been trained. An appalling lack of church historical studies is required of those in pastoral preparation. I have lost count of how many times graduates of seminaries have told me, upon first reading early Christian sources, that they had never been exposed to anything like it before. With a few exceptions, biblical and "practical" courses at free church seminaries crowd out the possibility of becoming more steeped in the church's formation and the historical struggles to define a Christian doctrine of God. What little is offered in historical theology usually consists of broad overviews of the church's two-millennial history, discussions of post-sixteenth-century themes and figures, or narratives of the denominational history of that Bible school or seminary. Like tiny footnotes in a large volume, the early centuries of the church's foundations have a minimalist place in the intellectual formation of students. Small wonder that evangelical and Protestant leaders still have little or no acquaintance with the patristic tradition or a sense that they should become acquainted with it.

The Point

Lest the title of the present book lead readers astray, this is not a book that seeks to defend tradition or its place within Christianity. Nor is there a need to do so. For nearly a millennium and a half, the Christian tradition has offered direction to believers of all communions and affiliations on how they should interpret the Bible, what they should know about God, and how to understand the essentials of Christ's person and work. The task here is much simpler: to show the origins of this tradition and how it was received as an authoritative guide by the earliest centuries of Christians. The intent of this book, therefore, is not to argue for the legitimacy of tradition but to illuminate its place within Christian thought and practice so that Protestants of all stripes can see the value and necessity of its resources for appropriating the faith today.

I am not talking about a revival of interest in historical Christianity. Simply telling readers that they need more church history in their intellectual diet is not the point. Rather, if contemporary evangelicalism aims to be doctrinally orthodox and exegetically faithful to Scripture, it cannot do so without recourse to and integration of the foundational tradition of the early church. Theological renewal for Protestantism in general and evangelicalism in particular will take place through an intentional recovery of Protestantism's catholic roots in the church's early spirituality and theology. Herein is an avenue that leads not to the loss of distinctiveness as Protestants but, as the sixteenth-century Reformers found, the resources necessary to preserve a Christian vision of the world and its unique message of redemption.

Because the Christian faith is always older and bigger than any one denominational claim upon it, we must examine more closely how the Christian tradition first developed in early Christianity. We need to see how it operated in relation to Scripture and the other principal doctrines of the sixteenth-century Reformation. Protestants should bear in mind that Protestantism is not a negative or reactionary understanding of Christianity. Only in a secondary sense is a Protestant one who "protests" (*protesto, -are*) against certain views of Roman Catholicism. In fact, a Protestant is by first definition one who affirms or professes the truths of the faith. For the first generation of Protestants, the truths of the faith were found in Scripture and the writings of the early church fathers.

Tradition: A Continuity of Faith?

It is particularly ironic, at least among academics, that while Protestant thinkers are looking more intensely for ways in which their faith is a continuation of earlier ages, contemporary Roman Catholic theologians are seeking ways to show how much doctrine and practice have changed throughout the centuries. Are there points along the continuum of the church's faith that connect today's Christianity with that of the early Christians? Evangelicals, who have paid little attention to the time between the era of the apostles and the Reformation, still assume that the answer is yes. To read the New Testament is to read about matters immediately relevant and applicable for today's church. While most of the church's history may be "fallen" and superfluous for maintaining a vital faith in the twenty-first century, the Bible as divine revelation does not suffer from the same limitations. Of course, such an antiseptic view of Christian history was challenged by Protestant liberal and moderate thinkers throughout the late nineteenth and twentieth centuries who concluded that the Bible is just as culturally and ideologically bound as the rest of church history. For most of theological liberalism,[4] however, this meant that the Bible as "story" ought to be distinguished from the Bible as "event." The "story" was central and had little to do with the actual facts of events. These events may

---

4. Another stream within Protestant liberalism took the approach that there is no substantial connection between what Christianity was and what it has become. Harvey Cox, for example, says that while we need to take lessons from the resources of the early Christians, we must avoid "mythicizing" them for our own purposes (Harvey Cox, *Turning East* [New York: Simon & Schuster, 1977], 160–61). Both story and events are pious fictions concocted by the earliest believers. For an overview, see J. Dillenberger and Claude Welch, *Protestant Christianity Interpreted through Its Development* (New York: Scribner's Sons, 1954).

or may not have actually occurred, but it did not really matter. The Christian "story," as portrayed in the apostles' writings and later patristic texts, was a decontextualized divine movement whose reality was not grounded in the variability of history. In the end, this meant that the grand narrative of Christianity had no actual continuity with the past; it was unhinged from the warp and woof of Christian history. Protestant fundamentalists and evangelicals responded by insisting on the complete continuity between "facts" and "story" as far as the Bible goes. Historical and cultural differences aside, believers may likewise count on a spiritual and doctrinal continuity between the time of the apostles and today, though this same principle is not applied to most of church history.

For hundreds of years, the official communiqués of the Vatican operated with a set of assumptions similar to that of evangelical Protestantism but for different reasons. Magisterial voices insisted that the church's tradition represents a more or less unchanging deposit of the Christian faith as articulated by the Roman Catholic Church. Not only is there a continuity of biblical or doctrinal truth from age to age, but the enduring nature of biblical and doctrinal truth is guaranteed only as it has been declared officially by the church. At the third session of the first Vatican Council (1870), the Vatican determined that while there is always progress in human understanding in the succession of ages, the meaning of "sacred dogmas is perpetually to be retained which our Holy Mother Church has once declared, and there must never be a deviation from that meaning."[5] This position was softened a century later when the Vatican said that all dogmatic formulations are historically conditioned and that the meaning of doctrinal pronouncements is always dependent upon changeable conceptions of the age in which a pronouncement is made. Longstanding teaching of the church may give way to new expressions, although the original meaning remains the same and remains binding.[6]

A large number of contemporary Roman Catholic theologians, however, are unhappy with what they regard as a dogmatic and

5. Cited in J. Neuner and J. Dupuis, eds., *The Christian Faith in the Doctrinal Documents of the Catholic Church* (New York: Alba House, 1995), 477. The *Constitution Orientalium Dignatis* (1894) stated in confirmation that the dogmas that the church has received have a divine character and therefore are immutable.

6. *Mysterium Ecclesiae* (May 11, 1973).

historically unsound response to the variegated nature of the church's traditions. Transmission of the tradition through time and place is susceptible to change, sometimes significantly so. Despite the openness expressed at Vatican II[7] regarding the inherent flexibility of the church's tradition, the official position is to view tradition as an object derived from the past that passes unchanged from one generation to the next.

Terrence Tilley, a Roman Catholic theologian, has made a cogent case to the contrary. His arguments are worth considering as a means for better understanding the present purpose of clarifying tradition. The problem, Tilley says, is that certain beliefs and practices deemed "traditional" by the church hierarchy are not found in the previous ages of the church in their present form or have no precedent at all. "If that which is passed on as a tradition has to be passed on 'unchanged and uncorrupted' over long periods of time, then there are no concrete traditions that will pass the test."[8] The last two millennia of church history have demonstrated that the church's tradition is in a constant state of adapting (or "inventing") itself to new theological, cultural, and linguistic changes such that tradition as content is not sufficient to explain the changes and innovations within tradition.

Instead, tradition should be understood as a set or network of enduring practices rather than a particular set of propositions. "Traditions are not reified 'things' that can be known apart from practice."[9] Religious practices are not self-evident and have to be interpreted by rules. Thus, Tilley argues for a "grammar of a tradition" or what he also calls a "rule theory of doctrine" that serves as a guide for determining legitimate or illegitimate developments

7. *Dei Verbum*, II.8, in *The Documents of Vatican II*, ed. W. Abbott (New York: Association Press, 1966), 116.

8. Terrence W. Tilley, *Inventing Catholic Tradition* (Maryknoll, N.Y.: Orbis, 2000), 27. Tilley minces no words about the reality of change in the church's official doctrine, as seen in the clear differences over the prerogative of religious freedom between the *Syllabus of Errors* (1864) and *Dignitatis Humanae* (1965). Movement from its condemnation in the nineteenth century to the advocacy of religious freedom at Vatican II as a positive political good constitutes a "reversal of principles" (ibid., 117). No developmental theory of doctrine could have anticipated the sort of radical change that occurred within the faith on this point. For church officials to declare otherwise is an abuse of tradition. Tilley singles out the Congregation for the Doctrine of the Faith, which has been an inventor, creator, or violator of the tradition it claims to preserve and defend (ibid., 38). This seems rather severe given the admissions in *Mysterium Ecclesiae*.

9. Ibid., 45.

of the tradition. Central to Tilley's argument is the constructed nature of tradition. Quite literally, tradition isn't anything if it isn't a construction. Most historians of Christianity would agree on this basic point. This is certainly one of the lessons that the fourth-century trinitarian controversies taught us. With a more objective eye, we see that both Arius and Athanasius were and were not representing the church's tradition in their theologies and that previous (Origenist) traditions had to undergo modification in the process of articulating a Nicene tradition. The ensuing polemics and characterizations of each figure by the opposing side were so harsh because there was no single agreed upon version of the tradition. What we call Nicene "orthodoxy" became the dominating theological tradition only after much time and internal strife.

The question is whether Tilley's "grammar of a tradition" is really able to help us determine the difference between authentic developments of tradition and illegitimate developments. Can rules of discourse about tradition enable believers to know whether a tradition is true as opposed to false? Even if we grant that unrealistic expectations have been placed on the content of tradition as an immutable and fixed entity, we must avoid the other extreme of saying that almost nothing can be said concretely about it, apart from the establishment of general "rules" of discourse. Accepting the mutable reality of tradition does not negate the idea that there exists within Christianity a core or central understanding that has enshrined itself in specific ways and continues to serve as a point of departure for subsequent theological and biblical exegesis. Like the incarnation itself, no element of the tradition is free from its own historical origins and context. Tilley is right to resist attempts to posit tradition in the abstract or Platonic ideal such that terrestrial traditions are derived from an ethereal tradition that is untouchable or unaffected by practices.

We may also ask whether the self-understanding of tradition has always been as static and immutable as moderns characterize it. The broader scope of catholicism offers evidence of something much less than a monolithic composition. For most of the early history of Christianity, there were at least two acknowledged sides to the tradition: (1) the apologetic-polemical, which sought to depict the tradition as linear and unchanging against heretical

claims of divine revelation, and (2) the interecclesial, which admitted the existence of a certain fringe or "loose ends" concerning
what the church teaches. Certainly, the rhetoric of each approach
to tradition impacted the other, but the two approaches are not
identical, distinguishing themselves in the primary literature.

Irenaeus is a good example of an ancient figure acquainted with
church politics who reveals this distinction. In his writing against
Gnosticism (*Against Heresies*), he presents the catholic faith in
monolithic style ("throughout the world the catholic church is one
body"), in complete agreement with itself and having an invari-
able succession of teaching. But in his intra-church activities, he
knows all too well of the differences that exist and result in divided
opinions.[10] A similar sort of distinction is found in the preface to
Origen's *First Principles*. Here the author is careful to differenti-
ate within the tradition or rule of faith between fundamental or
generally accepted expressions of the Christian faith and those
more debatable and controverted. Not all of what he would have
called tradition carried the same authority. Acknowledging such
diversity within early Christianity is not antithetical to positing
a central axis of faithful self-awareness that functioned within
the unfolding of sacramental activities and intellectual exchange
of living communities.

It is true that we can know the tradition only within the par-
ticularities of time and space, the reality of which should allow
for specific statements of belief, creeds, baptismal formulae, and
so on as reliable, if partial, manifestations of the tradition. No one
aspect of the early tradition can encapsulate the whole, nor should
it. The fact that there is no single embodiment of the tradition does
not mean that there are no specific embodiments that offer privileged guidance regarding how the tradition should look or operate.
The fact that the church's rule or tradition emerges from definite
times and spaces does not negate the same tradition's ability to
function as the chief hermeneutic for discerning the difference
between true and false doctrine. Even in its most enculturated
and hidebound forms, the ancient tradition offers true glimpses
of God's intention for our redemption and transformation into
the divine image.

10. Eusebius, *Ecclesiastical History* V.24.9–13.

Thus, the tradition manifested a fixed and fluid content within a living history, which, throughout the earliest centuries, was constituted by the church and also constituted what was the true church. Because the tradition has always functioned dynamically within the concrete moments of history, its essential character involves the duality of conservatism and change. In other words, we find within the operating domain of Christian tradition the joint imperatives of preservation and renewal. The former requires that the tradition be immune to the attrition of time, whereas the latter declares that its use is subject to abuse and corruption as well as recovery and correction.

For Clarification

For the purposes of this book, "tradition" or "traditions" refers to those elements of any Christian affiliation or denomination that govern its understanding. Every Protestant grouping has its traditions no matter how antitraditional and anticredal it may be. The very notions of biblical authority, the preeminence of Pauline theology in articulating the gospel, theories of believers' separation from the world, and so on all constitute kinds of traditions that evangelicals or fundamentalist Christians rely on for their approach to the Bible and the church. My primary interest, however, is in *the* tradition, the foundational legacy of apostolic and patristic faith, most accurately enshrined in Scripture and secondarily in the great confessions and creeds of the early church. More will be said about this in chapter 2.

Let me also define how I use the phrase "early church" (or "early Christian"). Essentially two applications of the label are used by scholars: as a reference to the Christian communities of the first and early second century, often called the New Testament church, or as a way of talking generally about patristic Christianity, that is, the period of the church that immediately followed the apostles and continued for five or six hundred years. I emphasize the latter as the early church, more or less equivalent with the patristic age.[11]

11. The term *patristic* (age of the ancient fathers) is really emblematic, referring to the early period of Christian literature, art, and history produced by men and women, orthodox and heretical, prominent and anonymous.

This is the era in which the formulation of Christian doctrine, canonization, and the interpretation of the Bible took place, making it "ground zero" for the way in which all subsequent ages of the church have defined themselves.

With regard to the structure of the present volume, the first chapter discusses the origination and basic components of the tradition as a preparation for what follows. Because tradition has so often posed problems for Protestants, much of this book deals with several major interpretive issues related to the authority of tradition (chap. 2) and the relationship between the tradition and the Protestant traditions of "Scripture alone" (chap. 3) and "by faith alone" (chap. 4). The capstone of these studies is a brief review of the ways in which the tradition was manifested within the diversity of the ancient sources (chap. 5).

Readers are encouraged to read the foundational sources for themselves. It is a needless though common mistake for newcomers to early Christian literature to be content with modern works that discuss this period instead of reading the sources themselves. Far worse is when teachers of church history do not mandate reading from these sources. Therefore, a short list of primary patristic texts in English follows the conclusion of this book. Baker Academic will also make available a collection of patristic texts that is meant to serve as a supplement to this book. For the nonspecialist in patristic studies, the sources listed there will be a good place to start. It is hoped that the pastor, professor, theology student, and informed lay reader will incorporate these sources into their respective ministries and spiritual quests.

CONVERSION
AND CONSTRUCTION

So that doctrine may influence numerous fields of human activity, with reference to individuals, to families, and social life, it is necessary first of all that the Church should never depart from the sacred patrimony of truth received from the Fathers.

Pope John's opening speech at Vatican II (1962)

HAD YOU CONVERTED to Christianity during the period that soon followed the apostles, you most likely would have come out of a Greco-Roman pagan worldview. This would have meant several things. In the first place, you were probably already very religious. When the apostle Paul said to the Athenians on Mars Hill (Acts 17) that he perceived they were steeped in religion, it was not a compliment but an observation. A veritable multitude of gods, spirits, *daemons*,[1] and philosophies were

---

1. The anglicized form of this word is *demons*, but demons (or *numina*, as the Latins called them) for the classical pagans were not necessarily negative in character. They could be benign, but they certainly were present and had to be reckoned with.

a practical part of daily pagan life. Roman culture was built on the understanding that the proliferation of religious activity was beneficial, not only for the person but (more importantly) also for the civic good. The philosopher-statesman Cicero had laid down the basis for right thinking about the welfare of society. *Pietas* (piety) or dutiful conduct in the amount of attention one paid to the gods by way of sacrifices, incense, and just plain lip service at public events was crucial for maintaining social stability. Everyone knew that the *pax Romana* was dependent on the *pax deorum* (peace of the gods). Even the religious skeptic must see, Cicero said, that "if our reverence for the gods was lost, we should see the end of good faith, of human brotherhood, even of justice itself."[2]

At the heart of religion was ritual, the kind and content of religious observances properly performed. Indeed, the Greco-Roman world was a strongly ritualistic culture that extended to virtually every area of one's life.[3] You and your family may have been worshipers of one god, be it a traditional god of the Roman pantheon or a more exotic god from Asia Minor such as Cybele, but you were not monotheists. Despite your personal devotion to Jupiter or Cybele, your weekly schedule demanded that you participate in the civic veneration of other gods, whether at your workplace, during a procession through your neighborhood, or at a banquet where a cup of libation was raised in honor of the emperor as a divine being. In such moments, you knew that these cultic acts[4] in the name of one god or another were social obligations and benefited the preservation of an ordered and secure life. From childhood you had been raised to be tolerant of this divine interchangeability. Even the loyalty to one's own family deity was not jeopardized by such religious syncretism. Accommodation to and assimilation of various divinities were the rule of the pagan life.

Of course, pagan religion also offered the hope of personal salvation. You would have heard of such phrases as "born again" or "baptism into new life" when it came to the spiritual benefits

2. Cicero, *On the Nature of the Gods* I.3.

3. Thomas Finn, *From Death to Rebirth: Ritual and Conversion in Antiquity* (Mahwah, N.J.: Paulist Press, 1997), 8.

4. In this context, *cultus* (a noun) means an activity of worship or veneration.

offered. Proponents of Cybele would have told you that to be re-born spiritually, you had to be bathed in streams of bull's blood, a ritual known as the taurobolium. But this really had nothing to do with allegiance to one God or a plurality of gods. In fact, salvation had little to do with the exact content of what you believed as long as you did the prescribed acts. Form and action, not content, were most important. After all, Socrates had shown that it was not important to believe everything behind the religious rites as long as you were involved in doing them.

In sum, this was a religious worldview that the classical historian A. D. Nock identified as salvation through "adherence."[5] You accrued religious benefit not by rejecting previous gods and former allegiances in order to embrace new ones but rather by accumulating multiple deities and participating in the various worship services offered to them. This was exemplified in Apuleius's novel *Metamorphosis* (second century), in which the main character, Lucius, was turned into a donkey for spurning the gods. Only after he participated in countless religious ceremonies and joined a solemn procession in honor of the goddess Isis did he resume his human form. Even after this event, he could be found at the temples of other gods just "to be on the safe side." There was no need to discard the former divinities in order to accept the benefits of new divinities. Again, accommodation and assimilation were the rule.

All of this began to change when you became a Christian, for becoming Christian meant *conversion*, not adherence. You could not simply add the God of Abraham and Moses to your menu of religious options. As with Judaism and some philosophical schools, converting to the Christian faith meant rejecting all previous religious attachments and allegiances to embrace the new. As Nock put it, "By conversion we mean the reorientation of the soul . . . a deliberate turning from indifference or from an earlier piety to another, a turning which implies a consciousness of great change is involved, that the old was wrong and the new is right."[6] Religious syncretism as an option was no longer acceptable. The radical nature of conversion was underscored by two elements

5. A. D. Nock, *Conversion: The Old and New in Religion from Alexander the Great to Augustine of Hippo* (Oxford: Oxford University Press, 1933).

6. Ibid., 7.

inherent to it: monotheism and the content of belief. Monotheism is defined by an unapologetic exclusivism that entails worship of one God as well as the rejection of all others. Converting to Christianity was like crossing the frontier into a completely different country: "an old spiritual home was left for a new once and for all."[7]

Conversion also meant that your religious activities were qualified by the assent of the mind and heart. In other words, the content of one's faith mattered; simply performing the right services was not enough. There was right teaching that led to salvation in Christ and to Christian maturity. When the apostle Peter proclaimed God's way of salvation through Jesus Christ to the Roman centurion Cornelius (Acts 10:34–43), his message contained a simple narrative of the death and resurrection of Christ and specific points of doctrine that provided the proper interpretation of the narrative. As a result of his resurrection, Christ is "the one whom God appointed as judge of the living and the dead" (v. 42), he is testified by the prophets (v. 43), and he provides "forgiveness of sins" to "whoever believes in him" (v. 43)—all doctrines that became standard features in the major creeds of patristic Christianity.

In proclaiming the kingdom, Jesus had already conjoined conversion and belief: "The time has come. . . . The kingdom of God is near. Repent and believe the good news!" (Mark 1:15). This fusion proved to be important for later generations of Christians because faith both as a response and as an intellectual content of the response became the pattern by which one's salvific experience was reinforced.[8] Christian conversion evidently called for major restructuring of the heart and mind, which required specific instruction and reinforcement of the salvation once begun. Baptism, prayer, liturgy, ethics, and the Eucharist (or Lord's Supper) all contributed to the Christianization of the individual. These elements were, in effect, venues by which a new believer was instructed in the faith. A late first- or early second-century document known to modern scholars as the *Didache* provides what may be the earliest manual of Christian instruction. It briefly tackles each of the essentials of Christian belief and practice: baptism,

7. Ibid.
8. Finn, *From Death to Rebirth*, 25.

prayer, celebrating the Eucharist, discerning true teachers from false, observance of the Lord's Day, appointment of leadership (bishops and deacons), and a list of commonly known key points of behavior (1.1–6.2) that lead to life or to death.[9]

In your new Christian life, you had no Bible as we understand the term today. Nothing like a standardized collection of texts existed, much less was available to believers. Many churches had copies of the Hebrew Bible translated into Greek known as the Old Covenant (Testament) by the mid-second century, though there were different versions that sometimes significantly conflicted with one another. At first, you would have wondered at the prominence of Jewish writings in a cosmopolitan religious movement. But you knew the value of prophecy from classical sources, given your cultural background, and had come to realize that the focus of these ancient prophecies was Christ. There was, of course, no New Testament yet. This did not mean, however, that you had no access to the apostolic writings. Evidence suggests that the Gospels (separate and together) and certain apostolic epistles circulated at the time. Other written works of Jesus' deeds and preaching likely existed,[10] but only some of these survived, and serious questions had been raised about their authenticity. More problematic was how an inauthentic apostolic writing was to be distinguished from an authentic one. There was no consensus on the matter as far as you could tell.

But all this did not matter much. Most Christians were functionally illiterate, which probably meant that you too learned your new religious devotion not through reading texts but in the way that Paul once stated: "Faith comes from hearing" (Rom. 10:17).[11] Christians valued the written word from the beginning and yet would have acquired the rudiments of the Christian faith through the early tradition as it was relayed via confessions, hymns, and baptismal instruction.

9. Known as the "Two Ways," this section seems to have had a wide circulation in Jewish and Jewish-Christian circles. Literary parallels are found in the *Manual of Discipline* from the Qumran (Dead Sea Scrolls) texts as well as in the Christian documents known as the *Epistle of Barnabas* and the fourth-century work known as the *Apostolic Constitutions*.

10. As Luke 1:1–2 implies.

11. Harry Gamble places the illiteracy rate of the general population of the Roman Empire at 90 percent or slightly less. See Harry Gamble, *Books and Readers in the Early Church: A History of Early Christian Texts* (New Haven: Yale University Press, 1995), 4–5.

The tradition had presented the preaching of the gospel long before written documents were at hand. Indeed, the written word served to confirm what had been preached and taught. Baptism was an especially important passage in the Christianization process, during which the Christian truth was learned, professed, and lived. One of the earliest examples of baptismal confession (early second century) recounts a believer's words:

> I believe in God, the Father Almighty,
> And in his only-begotten Son
>   Our Lord Jesus Christ,
> And in the Holy Spirit,
>   And in the resurrection of the flesh,
>   And in the holy catholic church.[12]

Like most confessions, the rock-bottom components of what makes belief pointedly *Christian* are presented in this short formula, one that was easy to remember and offered a basic structure for thinking about God. The tradition enabled new believers to be confronted with the knowledge that distinguished true faith from false, that revealed how to think about God rightly, and that showed them how to discern appropriate ways of personal and social conduct.

In sum, before Christians had a Bible of Old and New Testaments, they had the apostolic tradition, which led them through the steps of conversion, shepherded believers into the life of God—by the Father, through the Son, and in the Spirit—as realized within the church, helped them interpret the meaning of Scripture, and, when needed, supplied them with the word of hope in their suffering for Christ. The tradition was about salvation and how that salvation was nurtured once begun. The rest of this chapter looks at some of the mechanics of this tradition in its early stages.

Tradition in the Beginning

The language and earliest content of the Christian tradition were first articulated by the apostle Paul, who encouraged the Thessalonians to "stand firm and hold on to the traditions we

---

12. *Dêr Balyzeh Papyrus*, as cited in J. N. D. Kelly, *Early Christian Creeds*, 3rd ed. (London: Longman, 1972), 88.

passed on to you" (2 Thess. 2:15, author's translation). The apostle used the word *traditions* (Greek, *paradoseis*)[13] in its usual sense: a dynamic of handing over and receiving or a living and active transmission of the church's preaching. In this instance, his emphasis appears to be on ethical tradition, that is, corporate and personal Christian practices.[14] Most importantly, Paul does not set these traditions and his letter in opposition to each other. Rather, he sees them as complementary, as the remaining part of the verse shows: "Hold on to the traditions we passed on to you, whether by mouth or by letter." His epistle serves to confirm what the traditions had been teaching.

The same was true for his letter to the Corinthian church. By the time he wrote 1 Corinthians, the church already possessed a normative standard (the *paradosis*) (1 Cor. 11:2) concerning the "what" and "how" of the Christian faith. Using the vibrant language of tradition, Paul says he himself "received" (*paralambano*) this "gospel" from the Lord, which he also "delivered" (*paradidomi*) to his readers (1 Cor. 11:23; 15:3). The tradition in 1 Corinthians 11 has to do with order of worship, specifically celebrating the Lord's Supper. In 1 Corinthians 15, the tradition "of first importance" is a doctrinal one that enabled the Christians to interpret the Old Testament: "that Christ died for our sins according to the Scriptures, that he was buried, that he was raised on the third day according to the Scriptures, and that he appeared to Peter, and then to the Twelve" (vv. 3–5). Again, there is no perceived conflict between what the Corinthians had received by way of the church's existing tradition and the written epistle that would become Scripture.

It is important, moreover, to notice that in Paul's statements there is no tension between the gospel as revelation and the gospel as tradition. Revelation and the tradition were but two sides of one coin.[15] Thus, the tradition did not stand against the inspirational process, out of which emerged the New Testament; it was a critical means by which the risen Lord had imparted his revelation through the working of the Spirit.

From the earliest stages of the Christian church, therefore, the language of tradition became the modus operandi for expressing

---

13. Most unfortunately, the NIV translates this word as "teachings."

14. For a parallel, see Col. 2:6: "Just as you received [*paralambano*] Christ Jesus as Lord, continue to live in him."

15. F. F. Bruce, *Tradition: Old and New* (Grand Rapids: Zondervan, 1970), 31–32.

the transmission of the apostles' teaching, which was reflective of the Lord's own proclamation. As a result, Paul commands his readers to avoid any brother who "does not live according to the tradition [*paradosis*] you received [*paralambano*] from us" (2 Thess. 3:6). Both the noun and the verb of tradition language are used, in all likelihood, to stress that the activity of those who do not accept Paul's teaching is adverse not merely to him but also to the teaching of the whole church. A letter known as *1 Clement* makes the same application in its exhortation to the Corinthian Christians a half century after Paul. Rivalry over leadership had created dissension and schism in the congregation, and "Clement" urges anyone involved to give up such futile concerns and to "turn to the glorious and holy rule of our tradition" (7.2). The cumulative force of the tradition, not the writer, is the impetus for calling the church to such a response.

Unpacking the Meaning

There are several ways to understand the tradition as it first appears and begins to mature into different and more sophisticated forms. The evolution of the tradition does not have as much to do with the canonization of Scripture as it does with movements internal to the tradition itself. The French Roman Catholic scholar George Tavard has studied this phenomenon at great length, and from his writings three basic categories within tradition may be construed:[16] (1) tradition as transmission, (2) tradition and development, and (3) tradition as the memory of the church.

Tradition as transmission implies not only the act of transmitting but also, in an objective sense, *what* is transmitted. Unlike modern theology, which has become infatuated with understanding tradition as "process" and worries that attributing specific content to tradition might exclude a possible opinion or position, Tavard argues that the transmitted nature of the ancient tradition implies that a "something" is transmitted. This "something" of tradition is what Tavard calls the "continuum of fidelity" or the

16. What follows is indebted to the synthesis of Tavard's theology in Marc R. Alexander, "G. H. Tavard's Concept of Tradition," in *The Quadrilog: Tradition and the Future of Ecumenism*, ed. K. Hagen (Collegeville, Minn.: Liturgical Press, 1994), 287–311.

deposit of faith, and it embodies the message of the gospel and its theological interpretation.

Furthermore, to think of tradition as "handed over" is to designate tradition as something living. Reciting the Apostles' Creed or the Nicene Creed during worship is not merely repeating the past. It is recalling an experience or reliving an event. We make the creed come alive in the reciting, an act of faith by "remembering." "The creed provides the occasion and the immediate mechanism for the living expression of faith."[17] Obviously, it is possible to mouth the words of a creed in a faithless or dead way. In this case, the living tradition as received and its character as something transmitted are obviated.

A great deal has been written on doctrinal development as it relates to the variability of the content of tradition.[18] Simply put, the Christian tradition was and always is in the process of development. It is impossible to speak of passing on something unchanged. The reason for inevitable change is plain: Development is how the tradition responded to its present in light of its past. Transmission was not a matter of simply throwing ancient formulas or solutions at new problems and expecting them to be effective. Nor was it trying out new solutions without recourse to the resources of the existing tradition. Development, therefore, is not the introduction of changes but a response to discovering how the deposit of faith should function as a resource for the needs of the present. In this sense, Tavard says, tradition is not a guarantee. It was not an infallible process of delivering the true doctrine of the church. Since the transmission of faith is at all levels tied up with time, language, and culture, there is always change, and change is inherently imperfect. Holding firm to a doctrine of biblical inerrancy does not annul the changing vicissitudes of history or make the hermeneutical challenges of transmitting and interpreting meaning over the ages simply disappear. Confidence in the authenticity of the message transmitted to us across the ages must be placed in the God of history who promised to lead us into all truth. Protestants of every stripe must

---

17. Ibid., 289.

18. E.g., John Henry Newman, *An Essay on the Development of Christian Doctrine* (London: Longmans, Green & Co., 1903); Jaroslav Pelikan, *Development of Christian Doctrine* (New Haven: Yale University Press, 1969); and R. P. C. Hanson, *The Continuity of Christian Doctrine* (New York: Seabury Press, 1981).

place their confidence in the Lord of the church and trust that the essential tradition and Scripture are the sovereign work of the Holy Spirit operating in the earthly church. The delivering and receiving of tradition may not be an inerrant process, but it was built on the capacity of the word of our Lord to lead his disciples into all truth in the midst of the world (John 16:13), to enlighten the eyes of their hearts (Eph. 1:18), and to fill them with "the knowledge of his will through all spiritual wisdom and understanding" (Col. 1:9).

A valuable contribution Tavard has made to the debate over the meaning of tradition is his notion that tradition functions as the memory of the church. If tradition is a preserver of the church's faith as the work of God in the body of Christ, then it is supposed to be a living and shared memory. In this characteristic of tradition, we are directed to the role of the church, which harbors the tradition and is also the agent for handing the tradition over to new believers and to the world. Tradition as memory is not the work of the individual believer, although the believer participates in it, but of the corporate body of Christ, the church. Only within the church can memory reside each time the Lord's Supper is observed or a new Christian is baptized, when the memory of the faith is called back and reexperienced. In effect, the tradition has to do with how it is transmitted through the acts of the church.[19] As memory, tradition has to do with how the gospel is transmitted, how the divine presence is realized in the sacraments (or ordinances) among believers, and how lives are changed by Christian truth.

It is here where evangelicals and free church Christians are at greatest risk, because guarding the church's memory has little to do with the purposes that guide most contemporary worship services. Programmatic needs set the agenda for content and order more than a consciousness that the church's tradition as memory is essential for feeding the Lord's sheep. No doubt the trendy styles of worship and proclamation are attracting more people, but what are they being given once they come in the doors and stay? All the relational activity in the world cannot make up for an absence of a content grounded in the church's historical memory.

19. "It includes also the high moments of the successive existence of the church through the ages" (Tavard cited in Alexander, "G. H. Tavard's Concept of Tradition," 297).

Related to the absence of tangible reminders is a longstanding emphasis among free church congregations that spontaneity is a necessary ingredient for worship to be truly Spirit led. Whether through prayer, personal sharing, or the sermon, authenticity is best released through extemporaneous acts of faith. The implicit presupposition here is that spontaneity makes worship truly heart-felt. If the work and presence of the Spirit result in a believer's freedom (2 Cor. 3:17), earnest Christians should not resort to the wooden props of repetitive forms of words in worship.

In contrast, prayers offered at regular times of the Christian calendar year, liturgies, and collects are regarded with holy disdain as artificial works of piety. Unfortunately, too many Christians who harbor such antipathy have never been exposed to the Anglican Book of Common Prayer or a Roman Catholic missal, and therefore, they do not know the spiritual sensitivity, beauty, and depth that are often found in these "artificial" works.

Legitimation for the free church approach is thought to be warranted by direct parallels to Jesus' words about the disciples' future ministry: "Whenever you are arrested and brought to trial, do not worry beforehand about what to say. Just say whatever is given you at the time, for it is not you speaking, but the Holy Spirit" (Mark 13:11). Such spur-of-the-moment spirituality seems to have a greater holiness compared to prepackaged and predictable words taken from a prayer book or missal. Was not Jesus openly critical of religious leaders who thought they were heard "because of their many words" or "vain repetitions" (Matt. 6:7)? Yet Jesus was talking about an occasion when the sincerity of the heart does not match the piety of the words spoken, as opposed to the use of an ordered form of words thoughtfully used in worship. He would have been very familiar with and participated in the Jewish services of worship in the local synagogue, where the regular customs of congregational liturgies and commonly used prayers were observed.[20] Jesus was most critical of the hollowness of some practices of the Pharisees, not doing or understanding what they preached, rather than the worshipful traditions of the synagogue.

20. For the basic form of the synagogue liturgy as it probably was in Jesus' time, see Frank Senn, *Christian Liturgy: Catholic and Evangelical* (Minneapolis: Fortress, 1997), 68–70.

Spontaneous or planned, words spoken and deeds performed in worship may be for the wrong reasons and therefore have no merit. Worshipers may merely mouth the words of the liturgy or sing worship choruses with little or no shared sense of their meaning, which is not the fault of the words, whether they are preestablished or used on a whim. But there is nothing inherently artificial about the use of liturgies in worship services. While usually attached to ceremonial activities, the early use of the word *leitourgia* referred to various functions that were done for the public (i.e., congregational) good. Thus, Paul describes himself as a "liturgist of Christ Jesus to the Gentiles with the priestly duty of proclaiming the gospel to them" (Rom. 15:16, author's translation). As Paul was to the Gentiles, so Epaphroditus was to Paul when the latter was in prison. Writing to the Philippians, Paul refers to him as "your liturgist" (Phil. 2:25, 30) who ministered to Paul's needs. The term *liturgy* was again used by Paul to describe the collection of gifts by the churches in Macedonia and Greece for the relief of the believers in Jerusalem (1 Cor. 9:12). Jesus himself is called "a liturgist" in Hebrews 8:6, being the high priest of the new covenant as its mediator. Of course, Christ's role as liturgist was anything but spontaneous, having been planned before the creation of the world (1 Pet. 1:20). For believers who engage in liturgical ministry, whether as worship leaders or through acts of love, the point of importance is whether it is a truly spiritual service to God.

Ironically, the musical portion of services at many churches is preplanned and executed with meticulous attention to detail so that it is anything but spontaneous. Yet while the musical segments of contemporary worship services are expected to be carefully chosen and rehearsed, the use of a preplanned liturgy, on the other hand, is perceived as stiff, repetitious, and deadening.

There is nothing wrong with creating winsome programs for every age in a church, and yet congregational leaders must ask themselves the more vital question: How do their programs enable believers to discover the rich resources of the church's memory? How are neo-pagans of this age being Christianized such that their profession of salvation is truly a conversion? Surely the great promise of the gospel amounts to more than "accepting Jesus so that you'll go to heaven"!

In the resources of the tradition lie the essentials for Christian growth that are distinctively Christian, truly biblical, and doctrinally substantial. They are not the last word, so to speak, but they are the place for every Christian to begin in understanding the mind of the church. Drawing upon these resources allows believers to encounter and be encountered by the inheritance of catholic Christianity, the wholeness of the Christian faith that exceeds our tiny perspective of it. Not doing so is to risk nurturing Christians who are unable to stomach the "real food" of theology and sustained biblical reflection. Even worse, it invites the unconscious resurrection of old heresies in new guises.

Tradition and Christian Education

It is no accident that the earliest development of the ancient tradition emerged out of a situation of need. The early fathers most directly speak of the church's tradition in apologetic contexts (when they are defending catholic faith against its detractors) and when they are defining the faith (describing it for the needs of catechesis, that is, when they are explaining the faith in the context of instructing new believers for baptism). We ought to bear in mind that there were no systems yet designed for presenting the Christian faith, certainly no theological textbooks or Sunday school type of materials that offered a rudimentary outline of Christian belief and practice. When the second-century Christian philosopher Justin announced in his *Apology*[21] that he was offering a "reasoned" presentation of what Christians believe, he was making new inroads toward Christian self-definition. Thus, Christian theology as a "craft" sprang from the need to define the faith against error and to instruct new believers, both of which were done in accordance with the early tradition.

Defending the Faith

The surviving sources of the second and third centuries offer more evidence illustrating the apologetical and polemical side for

---

21. An *apologia* is a defense of one's position, based on Plato's apology for Socrates, who had been accused by the Athenian elders of corrupting the youth of the city with unconventional ideas.

defining the Christian faith than the catechetical. This is largely due to the fact that apologies were by nature public documents designed to teach openly the rationality of Christian belief and practice. Catecheses, however, having little formality for the first three centuries, were oral exercises meant for memorization, not print.

Although Justin ostensibly wrote his apology to the emperor (Antoninus Pius and his heirs) as well as cultured Roman pagans, the audience who benefited the most from the work was made up of Christian readers. This is not surprising since Justin was a catechist in the Roman church and was regularly involved in preparing new converts for baptism. After addressing the charges laid against Christians (atheism, immorality, etc.), Justin proceeds to discuss Christian belief, virtues, and worship practices all the while supporting his arguments from Scripture (mainly the Old Testament). This latter characteristic of his treatise suggests that Christian believers were the implicitly intended audience. It is hard to imagine that Roman intellectuals would have placed any value on Christian Scriptures as sources of religious authority. Still, they were not oblivious to this literature. The pagan philosopher Celsus was probably motivated to write his anti-Christian book *The True Discourse* (in the early third century) by Justin's apology.

Defining the Faith

The notion of a catechumenate—a series of steps that leads a new believer to baptism and a deeper knowledge of the faith—was a creation of the early fathers who also gave shape to its integral role within Christian experience. This was, in effect, the first version of Sunday school, though a temporary schooling with specific aims. The earliest evidence for the process indicates that it varied from place to place and that it was fairly simple (e.g., the instructions given in the *Didache*). A more elaborate system was found in Rome as described in the *Apostolic Tradition* by Hippolytus, an elder and bishop-hopeful in the church there. But the Roman process was probably not the norm, and most other churches, being in smaller towns or rural settings, had something simpler.

Catechesis, or Christian instruction for new believers, reached new heights in the fourth century. Greater doctrinal sophistica-

tion due to the trinitarian and christological debates, the rise
of several generations of highly educated and erudite Christian
thinkers, and the influx of new Christians following the end of
persecution led to more carefully and consistently defined structures for Christianizing converts.[22] This emphasis provides many
examples of how the tradition took shape in this period and its
role in Christian education.

The seriousness with which Christian leadership addressed
pre-baptismal instruction is stated succinctly in the following
directions:

> Let him, therefore, who is to be taught the truth in regard to piety
> be instructed before his baptism in the knowledge of the Unbegot-
> ten God, in the understanding of His Only-begotten Son, in the
> assured acknowledgment of the Holy Spirit. Let him learn the order
> of the several parts of the creation, the series of providential acts,
> the different workings of God's laws.
>
> Let him be instructed about why the world was made, and why
> man was appointed to be a citizen in it; let him also know about
> his own human nature, of what sort of creature he is; let him be
> taught how God punished the wicked with water and fire, and
> glorified the saints in every generation . . . and how God did not
> reject mankind, but called them from their error and vanity to
> acknowledge the truth in various stages of history, leading them
> from bondage and impiety to liberty and piety, from injustice to
> justice, from death eternal to everlasting life.[23]

The unknown writer's intention is clear enough. New Christians
should become acquainted with the truths about God's identity
as Father, Son, and Spirit and that the one God is truly a Trinity. This God and no other being or force created and orders the
world, and his laws have given guidance throughout history and
are tailored for each stage. Converts should discover the truth
about their own dependent nature and that they stand responsible before God for not following after the good and the true.
More will be said in chapter 5 about the later developments in
catechetical instruction.

22. William Harmless, *Augustine and the Catechumenate* (Collegeville, Minn.: Liturgical Press, 1995), 51–56.

23. *Apostolic Constitutions* 7.39.1–4 (translation slightly altered).

The Catholic Faith

A final element of the tradition that should be noted here is its catholicity. Protestants of all stripes must comprehend once and for all that "catholic" is not the opposite of "Protestant." Especially evangelicals and free church believers should understand that the catholic faith is that which they also regard as the true faith. It has been stated often before,[24] but let it be observed here also that "catholic" does not equal Roman Catholicism and that catholicism as a concept and an identity defining orthodox Christianity was articulated early in the church's history. Catholicity is no less necessary for sustaining the future integrity of Protestant identity than it is for grounding Roman Catholicism. Protestantism is as dependent upon the history of the early church for its identity as any other Christian communion. No single communion can claim to be sole possessor of the *catholica,* while every Christian church is invited to identify itself with its depths and the riches of its good guidance.

Early in the first decade of the second century, Ignatius of Antioch used the adjective *catholic* in a way that shows it was already in use among churches in the East. This first appearance of the word as a conscious term of description also shows that it was indissolubly linked with the church as the corporate body of Christ: The congregation that made up the church of Smyrna was "the Catholic church" in terms of the mutual presence of the bishop (pastor), the congregation, and Jesus Christ.[25] In other words, "catholic" is that which qualifies the apostolic church, wherein is the living presence of Christ. There is not an emphasis here on catholic as "universal" in a spatial or empirical sense. A younger contemporary, Polycarp, a reputed disciple of John the apostle and bishop of Smyrna, is said to have prayed on the day of his martyrdom for "all the catholic church," which he states is "throughout the world."[26] Yet the same document refers to the single church at Smyrna as "the Catholic church" (16.2).

24. For a short study of the historical use of the term and concept, see appendix 1, "Why All Christians Are Catholics," in D. H. Williams, *Retrieving the Tradition and Renewing Evangelicalism: A Primer for Suspicious Protestants* (Grand Rapids: Eerdmans, 1999).

25. Ignatius of Antioch, *Epistle to the Smyrnaeans* 8.2 ("catholica ecclesia").

26. *Martyrdom of Polycarp* 8.1.

As a noun, the word *catholic* stresses the two components of the Greek word *kat-holou,* meaning "wholeness" or "entirety." The church catholic teaches the whole counsel of the gospel, meaning nothing in its message regarding salvation and sanctification is lacking. Catholicity is the unity found in the Lord's teaching, a wholeness of a *via vitae:* belief, worship, and morals.[27] It is the communion of orthodoxy (lit., right opinion) as contrasted with Christian sectarianism (e.g., Gnosticism) or paganism. This kind of meaning attributed to catholicity is found in the more profound modern treatments of catholicism by Henri de Lubac and Karl Adam.[28] Rather than defining catholicism *per se,* both writers engage in discussions about how doctrine, the church, the sacraments, interpreting Scripture, and so on intersect with one another and together form the catholic identity. Catholicity, by its very nature, is characteristic of *what* the church professes and does. The wholeness of the catholic faith is found in the wholeness of the church's life.

For over a millennium and a half, Christians in all parts of the world (Protestant, Roman Catholic, and Eastern Orthodox) have confessed with some variation that the essence of true faith includes belief in "one holy catholic church."[29] The very concept of catholicity as universality transcends both space and time. The church catholic is everywhere it ought to be and has been through each age since Christ. It is reasonable, therefore, to think that catholicity offers the best chance for achieving ecumenicity. Modern theologians are correct in saying that ideas about catholicity need to be expanded beyond the borders of denominational worlds and constraints. De Lubac noted that the universality of catholicism is the opposite of a closed society.[30] Not that we should confuse this universality with the church's outward form. The church is catholic not merely because it

---

27. R. N. Flew and R. E. Davies, eds., *The Catholicity of Protestantism* (London: Lutterworth Press, 1950), 23.

28. Henri de Lubac, *Catholicism: Christ and the Common Destiny of Man,* trans. L. C. Sheppard and E. Englund (San Francisco: Ignatius Press, 1988); and Karl Adam, *The Spirit of Catholicism,* trans. J. McCann, rev. ed. (New York: Image Books, 1954).

29. As one finds in the writings of Cyril of Jerusalem and Epiphanius of Salamis and in the Apostles' Creed and the Athanasian Creed. The Creed of Constantinople (381) contains the fourfold descriptive of the church, "one, holy, catholic, and apostolic," that became the normative confession for many Protestant bodies.

30. De Lubac, *Catholicism,* 298.

unites all members and all local churches in every act and event of Christ's life. Catholicity, rather, is oneness in the Holy Spirit, and this unity is the highest wholeness and fullness.[31]

Moreover, catholicity as universal in scope is not the same thing as promoting universalism. The invitation of catholicism to embrace the world should not be confused with a radical inclusivism captivated by a culture of overbearing pluralism and confused tolerance.[32] As John Wesley remarked in his sermon on the catholic spirit, it is not "speculative latitudinarianism."

> It is true that one should always be ready to hear and weigh whatsoever can be offered against his principles; but as this does not show any wavering in his own mind, so neither does it occasion any. He does not halt between two opinions, nor vainly endeavor to blend them into one.[33]

Not every doctrine or practice dubbed "Christian" or "biblical" can be included under the broad umbrella of catholicism. For something to be just or true or beautiful means that its contraries cannot also be right. Catholicity is not merely or even primarily about our irenic approaches to existing differences. It has more to do with the substance of our faith, "the true faith, the right faith, the catholic faith."[34]

Catholicism cannot be reduced to doctrinal or moral propositions, as some theologians fear is too often the case. But catholicity does imply that parameters exist for defining beliefs and practices that are truly Christian. In the third paragraph of the Athanasian Creed, it is plainly stated: *"Fides autem catholica haec est"* (And the catholic faith is this). Catholic tradition did and does possess a *receptum,* something specifically received by a believer or a congregation that distinguishes it as cleaving to faithful Christianity.[35] The *receptum* is what maintained continuity and linked

---

31. George Florovsky, *Bible, Church, Tradition: An Eastern Orthodox View* (Belmont, Mass.: Nordland, 1972), 41.

32. For an explanation of this mistake, see D. H. Williams, "The Diffusive Disintegration of Catholicity," *Pro Ecclesia* 23 (2003): 289–93.

33. John Wesley, *Sermon* 39.3.1.

34. Augustine, *Sermon* 52.2.

35. A partial working definition of essential catholicism, for example, can be found in the recent restatement of *Ex Corde Ecclesiae,* which argues for a shared baptismal belief in the truths that are rooted in Scripture and tradition, as interpreted by the church,

Christians to the Christian legacy of the past. Usually this was something basic such as a baptismal confession, which was the means by which "Christians recognize each other."[36] This was, in turn, the basis for unity and understanding.

The early church's emphasis on the catholic tradition further qualifies the sort of tradition we are talking about. In itself, there is nothing sacrosanct about "tradition." Many religious traditions exist today that are regarded as valuable and worthy of preserving, just as was the case eighteen hundred years ago, but they are not fundamentally Christian traditions. In the late second century, Irenaeus noted in his anti-heretical writing that church communities existed in the town of Lyons, where he was pastor, but not all of them were catholic. Apparently, diverse groups referred to themselves as true Christians and claimed to have a true knowledge of God that set them apart from the world and other ("carnal") Christians. These communities used the Old Testament and whatever writings of the New Testament that they possessed. The lure of acquiring special spiritual insight and scriptural understanding was of course attractive to these movements, often known by the blanket term *Gnosticism*. It was necessary for Irenaeus to stipulate the basis of catholic Christianity, which was distinguished by its apostolic character according to the rule (or canon) of faith and by the way that truly apostolic churches were interconnected with churches founded by the apostles or disciples of apostles. Direct and special knowledge from "on high" did not necessarily mean that a church preached the gospel of truth.

Thus, that which was "catholic" had to do with those most fundamental truths of the Christian faith according to Scripture that bound Christians together. The notion of "wholeness" was not the attainment of unity regardless of traditional norms of doctrinal or moral integrity. Augustine makes this plain when he describes the features of what he calls "true religion."

---

concerning the mystery of the Trinity: God the Father and Creator, who works even until now; God the Son and incarnate Redeemer, who is the way and the truth and the life; and God the Holy Spirit, the Paraclete, whom the Father and the Son send ("*Ex Corde Ecclesiae*: An Application to the United States," *Origins* 29 [1999]: 404).

36. Augustine, *Sermon* 213.2.

This is the catholic church, strongly and widely spread throughout the world, making use of all who are in error in order to correct them if they are willing to be awakened, which is a way of assisting the church's own progress. It makes use of the nations as material for its own operations; of heretics as a means of testing its own teaching; of schismatics to prove its own stability. . . . Some it invites, others it excludes, some it leaves behind, others it leads. To all it gives the power to participate in the grace of God.[37]

The *catholica* is the teaching of the New Testament and the early fathers that is common to churches that profess the historic Christian faith. It is the guarantee that God loves and saves us and tells us about himself.

---

37. Augustine, *On True Religion* vi, 10.

THE EARLY CHURCH
AS CANONICAL

In accordance with the apostolic faith delivered to us by tradition from the Fathers, I have delivered that tradition without inventing anything extraneous to it. What I have learned, that is what I have written down, in conformity with the Holy Scriptures.

Athanasius of Alexandria, *Letter to Serapion*

NOT ALL TRADITION is equal. For almost two millennia, the church's tradition has provided Christians with the essential baseline of theological faithfulness. But it has not always been clear which elements of the tradition should serve as ongoing standards for Christianity and which are denominationally or culturally specific. Since the sixteenth century, one of the persistent conflicts among Protestants, Roman Catholics, and Greek Orthodox has involved how one should discern which aspects of traditions are normative and which are not.

Constructive and interchurch dialogue on the matter of tradition was not taken up until the Faith and Order conferences (of the World Council of Churches) held at Lund, Sweden (1952), and Montreal (1963). A report from Lund proposed "further ecumenical discussion to be found in that common history we have as Christians and which we have discovered to be longer, larger, and richer than any of our separate histories in our divided churches."[1] The studies produced at Montreal permanently altered the way in which modern theology thought about tradition. Especially important at this conference was that Eastern Orthodoxy was central to the discussions and helped broaden the concept of tradition in fruitful ways. A threefold way of clarifying tradition was proposed at Montreal: (1) "Tradition" chiefly refers to the activity of tradition (the dynamic of traditioning) by which a specific content of faith is transmitted; (2) "traditions" denotes the diversity of concrete manifestations of the traditioning process, namely, the various church affiliations or denominations; and (3) "the Tradition" is the common life of the church that has its source in God's act of revelation in Jesus Christ, the work of the Holy Spirit in his people, and his work in their history. The rationale for positing "the Tradition" was that the plurality of traditions presupposes a kind of identity and continuity that links them together. All major Christian traditions must "point beyond themselves to a common source and head."[2]

I too have followed a similar path of distinguishing *the* tradition from traditions along the lines just described.[3] As mentioned in the preface of this book, friendly critics of my previous work on tradition commented on how I attributed tradition chiefly to the patristic period. My way of seemingly limiting the meaning of the term has been viewed as problematic. Surely if tradition is an active and progressive movement within the life of the church, we should be able to talk about how tradition is articulated and shaped in each age. As a living entity, the tradition acts as a creative force within the Christian faith, which means it is subject to

1. *The Third World Conference on Faith and Order* (London: SCM, 1952), 27. Cf. K. E. Skydsgaard, "Tradition as an Issue in Contemporary Theology," in *The Old and the New in the Church*, World Council of Churches Commission on Faith and Order (Minneapolis: Augsburg, 1961).

2. "The Report of the Theological Commission on Tradition and Traditions," *Faith and Order Paper*, no. 40 (Geneva: World Council of Churches, 1963), 17–18.

3. D. H. Williams, "Reflections on *Retrieving the Tradition and Renewing Evangelicalism*: A Response," *Scottish Journal of Theology* 55 (2002): 105–12.

expansion and reform in its development. My Roman Catholic brethren are especially keen to insist on the ability of tradition to speak to each new generation and to be reinterpreted for the needs of the church in every age.[4] This is a valid and fruitful way to think of tradition, the utility of which I have acknowledged.

The Montreal definition, however, is seeking an even broader definition, equating the tradition with the whole history of salvation, God's message of redemption transmitted across the ages in and by the church.[5] The problem with the Montreal definition is that it ultimately suffers from the Platonic syndrome. The tradition becomes a kind of idealized form of every but no one tradition, a suprahistorical vision of the church's life through time with no concrete connection to time. It has an unmistakable appeal to content,[6] distinguishing it from the act of tradition but without providing incarnate standards of content. The tradition is not merely an essential "act" throughout historical times. It possesses a content in particular times that can be grasped utterly, though not entirely, in earthly terms and contexts.

Comprising a dynamic character in history, the tradition is not limited by any one culture, generation, language, etc. This is what some modern theologians mean by the phrase "the great tradition," a trajectory of doctrinal faithfulness that has been uncovered in the course of the patristic, medieval, and Reformation periods. After all, Protestants want to defend the influx of traditions lately brought into church history by Protestantism such as *sola fide*, the egalitarian priesthood of all believers, and ecclesial voluntarism. Should there not always be room for the

1. See *Dei Verbum*, II 8–10, in *The Documents of Vatican II*, ed. W. Abbott (New York: Association Press, 1966), 115–18. The Vatican is committed to a progressive view of tradition in support of its view of the ongoing revelatory nature of tradition. The prospect of new revelation is denied explicitly in both the "Dogmatic Constitution on the Church" and the "Dogmatic Constitution on Divine Revelation." These statements notwithstanding, article 8 seems to suggest the possibility of hitherto undisclosed public revelations being discovered. A good critique is found in E. G. Hinson, "The Authority of Tradition. A Baptist View," in *The Free Church and the Early Church: Essays in Bridging the Historical and Theological Divide*, ed. D. H. Williams, 141–61 (Grand Rapids: Eerdmans, 2002).

5. P. C. Rodger and L. Vischer, eds., *The Fourth World Conference on Faith and Order: Montreal 1963* (New York: Association Press, 1964), 50.

6. E.g., "all the manifold traditions of the past and present are under the judgment of the Tradition" ("Report of the Theological Commission on Tradition and Traditions," 18).

correction of traditions or new understandings of the gospel to be incorporated into the tradition?

At the same time, the incorporation of subsequent traditions or the reform of tradition has come about on the basis of an appeal to an earlier, foundational tradition that has operated as the norm. Faithfulness in the development of tradition is the degree to which the latter stands in relation to the primordial deposit of tradition. Protestants would therefore agree that not all dogmatic declarations should be regarded as tradition, such as the doctrine of papal infallibility or Mary's bodily ascension to heaven. All earthly traditions can claim to be genuine forms of the Christian faith only to the extent that they mirror in a consensual way *the* tradition.

Thus, I wish to designate the tradition in a manner more circumscribed than the Montreal statement, applicable chiefly to the apostolic and patristic faith. The basis of all tradition that originated in the apostolic and postapostolic centuries offers not a uniform or purist picture of the church but the theological and confessional building blocks on which ensuing Christian thought, practice, worship, and so on have been built. The tradition may not be reduced to the early church, but it certainly includes it and is largely defined by it. As such, the tradition is the various incarnations of the Christian faith articulated during the first five or six centuries.[7] In real and tangible ways, this period has functioned like a "canon" of Christian theology (doctrine, liturgy, prayer, exegesis, etc.) and has been the basis for directing the subsequent course of theology. In other words, the apostolic and patristic tradition is foundational to the Christian faith in *normative* ways that no other period of the church's history can claim. A theologian or pastor may agree or disagree

---

7. Scholars place the end of the patristic era between the fifth century and the seventh century. There is no agreement on this because no one definitive event or author marks the end. The best way to indicate the close of the "age of the fathers" is when writers begin to look backward in time for religious authority rather than to the present when it comes to validating their arguments. While the ancient Christians always regarded the past with high esteem, one can point to an increasing number of instances in the late fifth and six centuries when writers thought of the earlier fathers as privileged witnesses to Christian truth. This is, like all alternatives, quite subjective, and exceptions to it can be found. It does more justice, however, to the nuances required for the various factors of historical interpretation. See Patrick Gray, "'The Select Fathers': Canonizing the Patristic Past," *Studia Patristica* 23 (1989): 21–36.

with the patristic legacy, but it is functioning nonetheless as a rule by which such agreement or disagreement occurs. Even from a postmodern orientation, which refuses to identify with any standard of faith as an enduring standard, all theologizing is still done using a terminology and a conceptuality that are beholden to established norms of the Christian past and shape the direction of the future.[8]

The above "canonical" understanding of the tradition does not violate the continuing character of traditions within the body of Christ, although this way of describing the tradition is privileging the earliest stages of tradition (apostolic and patristic) over all later forms. As stated at the outset of this chapter, not all tradition is equal. With that in mind, it should also be said that the tradition in its apostolic phase, developing under the active influence of the Lord and the apostles under the direct guidance of the Holy Spirit, has priority over the manifestations of the tradition in the patristic church. For this reason, Scripture possesses a normativity that is superior to the tradition. But it is no less true that the church of Christ has always depended on the way in which the former has been mediated through the latter.

The most familiar example of the patristic age as canon is how the Apostles' and Nicene creeds have remained theological and ecclesiastical guideposts for signaling the way of orthodoxy for the Christian faith. Even for those church communions that do not regularly profess these creeds or acknowledge them in worship, the faith of these churches is dependent upon the theology that the major creeds represent. By and large, nearly every evangelical and free church congregation is taught theology consistent with or approximate to a Nicene trinitarianism and a Chalcedonian Christology. The raw material for such teaching may be from the New Testament, but the doctrines are patristic. Of course, the patristic canon is not able to comprehend the whole of the Christian faith—it never could   but it does present fundamentally and definitively what constitutes the "Christian" of the Christian faith.

8. See Lieven Boeve, *The Interruption of Tradition: An Essay on Christian Faith in a Postmodern Context* (Grand Rapids: Eerdmans, 2003).

Apostolic and Patristic

Applying the vocabulary of "canon" and "canonical" to the apostolic *and* patristic theological tradition may raise the eyebrows of some readers. My intent in doing so is not to be provocative by taking a controversial approach to the subject. By signaling the normative status of the patristic tradition, I am seeking to do several things at once. First, I want to emphasize the indissoluble connection that existed between the apostolic and the patristic church. The two should indeed be distinguished, the apostolic representing the voices of those who were the first disciples and hearers of the Lord. But far too often we take the artificial boundaries established in textbooks for purposes of clarifying the stages in church history as real divisions. Calling the time of the apostles "apostolic" and what followed "catholic" has served not only to distinguish the latter period as postapostolic but also to depict it as a series of developments not in keeping with the original apostolic charter. As the influential church historian Adolf von Harnack of the last century would have it, the apostolic reliance on the gifts and freedom of the Spirit was transformed into the fixing of tradition and doctrinal content known as "catholicism," in which a "canon of faith" eclipsed the spiritual simplicity of Jesus.[9] But it is one thing to observe changes of development and quite another to create a disjunction. One can point to a formation of doctrinal tradition in the earliest apostolic writings and dependency upon the Spirit's leading in later patristic texts. A strict delineation between the apostolic and the patristic is no more than a theoretical construct that fails at integrating the historical evidence. The manual of Christian practice and worship known as the *Didache* originated in the area of northern Syria, as did the Gospel of Matthew, and was produced within a generation or less of the Gospel.[10] *First Clement* was written, just like Revelation, in the mid 90s of the first century. Yet one was eventually regarded as apostolic and the other patristic. The

9. Adolf von Harnack, *History of Dogma*, vol. 2, trans. N. Buchanan (New York: Dover Publications, 1961), 25.

10. Matthew's Gospel is closely associated with Antioch, whereas the *Didache*, at least in its final form, seems to come from a more rural area of Syria. See R. E. Brown and J. P. Meier, *Antioch and Rome: New Testament Cradles of Catholic Christianity* (New York: Paulist Press, 1982), 81–84.

reasons for this distinction are not always apparent, underscored by the evidence that *1 Clement* and the *Didache* were regarded as Scripture (as were some other patristic works) by certain churches. The distinctions we so readily make today between apostolic and patristic were not clear to the Christians who were living in those times.

Second, advocating the normativity of the patristic faith in addition to the apostolic is merely giving voice to the theological and historical ramifications that have already been operating for over a millennium. Again, it may be that many Protestant and evangelical churches have rarely or never expressed the rudiments of this tradition in a formal manner (i.e., in worship), though they often exhibit a knowledge, however oblique, of the inheritance of the early church. However, the appropriation of the patristic legacy is nowhere more evident than in the Christian canonical collection known as the New Testament. The scope and extent of the Bible were realized by the patristic church, which discerned what was Scripture according to criteria of apostolicity, inspiration, and so on. Even the theological concept of apostolicity was not fashioned into a principle of authority until the mid-second century. Polycarp, the bishop of Smyrna who laid down his life for the Christian witness, is called in the account of his martyrdom "an apostolic and prophetic teacher." He had always preserved and transmitted faithfully the teaching given to him by the apostles.[11] That which is apostolic, or apostolicity, was a developed idea mainly pertaining to the conservation and continuation of what the apostles taught.[12] With good reason did George Florovsky declare, "The Church is apostolic indeed, but the Church is also patristic,"[13] that is, faithfulness to the gospel was first defined and lived out by those we call the fathers of the church.

11. *Martyrdom of Polycarp* 16.2; Irenaeus, *Against Heresies* III.3, 4.

12. The word *apostolic* is first used in Ignatius of Antioch's preface to his letter to the Trallians (c. 117) in reference to the imitation of a personal model, but Irenaeus provides us with what would become the standard understanding: "The church . . . has received from the Apostles and their disciples the faith." He then proceeds to give a summary of that faith (Irenaeus, *Against Heresies* I.10).

13. George Florovsky, *Bible, Church, Tradition: An Eastern Orthodox View* (Belmont, Mass.: Nordland, 1972), 107.

Scriptural and Theological Canons

Before we go any further, more qualification is in order. Let me reiterate that "canon" is any mechanism for standardizing a measurement or an evaluation. Speaking figuratively in a Christian context, the canon is a fixed norm or rule for determining the parameters of Christian thought and life. It has nothing necessarily to do with a list(s) of texts. Even if we were talking about texts, a given writing may be regarded as authoritative, even inspired, but it may not (or not yet) belong to an authoritative body of literature considered canonical. Examples of this from the first- and second-century corpus known as the Apostolic Fathers have been well documented.[14] Within the New Testament itself, one can point to the prophecy of Enoch in Jude 14. It is apparent that the writer of Jude is using *1 Enoch* (60:8), an oft-used Jewish apocalyptic text, as an inspired text, introducing it by the term *prophesied.* Many Jews and Christian Jews considered the text of *1* and *2 Enoch* "God-breathed" (i.e., inspired). Modern Christian readers may be disturbed by such a citation if they assume that inspiration was equivalent to canonicity at this early date.

The more familiar meaning of "canon" refers to a fixing of authoritative religious texts into a standardized body. Yet we must recognize that both narratives and texts were often acknowledged as authoritative within Christian churches long before they were placed, if at all, into fixed and standardized formats.[15] The book of Eldad and Modat, an otherwise unknown Jewish apocalyptic text (whose name seems to be taken from Num. 11:26–27), is quoted by the *Shepherd of Hermas* with the introductory words "it is written,"[16] yet the book does not appear in any early collection of canonical writings. Interestingly, the *Shepherd,* also an apocalyptic text from the early second century, became popular in

14. *The Epistle of Barnabas* begins a quotation from *2 Enoch* (89.5) with "the Scripture says" (16.5); *2 Clement* (11.2) cites *1 Clement* 23.3 with the words, "For the prophetic word also says."

15. A readable presentation of the nuances within the word *canon* are found in Lee M. McDonald, *The Formation of the Christian Biblical Canon* (Peabody, Mass.: Hendrickson, 1995). He utilizes Gerald Sheppard's dual distinction of "canon I" and "canon II." The first refers to a rule or standard that is followed whether in oral or written form, whereas "canon II" designates a collection of writings that are permanently fixed.

16. *Shepherd, Vision* 2.7, 4. Two other possible references to the same work are from *1 Clement* 23.3 and *2 Clement* 11.

certain Christian circles and was listed as Scripture in the preeminent biblical codex Sinaiticus (from the fourth century).[17] Rather like today, apocalyptic reading had a wide appeal. The *Shepherd*, therefore, despite its questionable doctrine, was regarded as an authoritative and inspired text for several centuries. Despite all this, the *Shepherd* was not ultimately regarded as canonical.

Of course, the term *canon* is most used for those books of Scripture that the church has recognized to be divinely inspired and therefore authoritative for Christian faith and practice. When students of theology or divinity hear of the "canon," they are taught to think of the biblical texts. What is not so commonly understood is that, while the New Testament was written by apostles and the earliest followers of Christ in the first century, its formation into a concrete and recognized collection, along with the Old Testament,[18] was a uniquely patristic accomplishment. That is, the means by which the biblical books were regarded as inspired and divinely given for Christian doctrine and practice took place in the postapostolic centuries of the early church. This process was a gradual and untidy one that emerged out of the worship and liturgical practices of the early churches. But just as importantly, it should be understood that the very concept of "canon" was first applied to the church's profession of faith, not to a list of authoritative texts. What the church *believed* was canonical long before that belief took written, codified forms. In fact, the earliest canons or norms of the preaching and defending of the early tradition served as the standard for the canonization of texts. Handbooks on the canonization of Scripture usually refer to this feature as the characteristic of apostolicity or orthodoxy and place it among the criteria of how books of the Bible became regarded as canonical.[19] While more than one principle was at work in the canonization process, the resemblance of a book's theological

17. Irenaeus, Tertullian, Clement of Alexandria, and Origen all cite the *Shepherd* as authoritative.

18. Not until the end of the second century was the phrase "Old Testament" used as a way of distinguishing it from the "gospel and apostle." The earliest known usage is in the *Book of Extracts* of Melito of Sardis, a document quoted by Eusebius of Caesarea (*Ecclesiastical History* IV.26.12) and known only in fragmentary form. There was no firm agreement on the parameters of the content of the old covenant and even less regarding what would become the New Testament.

19. F. F. Bruce, *The Canon of Scripture* (Downers Grove, Ill.: InterVarsity, 1988); and McDonald, *Formation of the Christian Biblical Canon*, 229–36.

content to the church's canon of faith was undoubtedly more important than any other factor. The *Shepherd of Hermas* eventually disappeared from scriptural canonical collections because it was too far removed from the essential points of the tradition.

Thus, the faith articulated during the first five centuries set in place two pillars of authority on which Christians have stood: (1) an apostolic canon of Scripture (the Bible) and (2) a theological canon of apostolicity (cardinal doctrines and confessions of the Trinity, Christology, etc.). The first has to do with the process of codifying the collection of the New Testament, which stands alongside the Old Testament. In other words, gospel and apostle are never supposed to function severed from the prophets. Jesus' words to the disciples along the Emmaus road in Luke 24 served as the archetype for this axiom. The second, a theological canon of apostolicity, refers to the forms in which the early church laid down the baseline of essential Christian truths: confessions, creeds, doctrines, interpretations of the Bible, hymns, and so on. Scripture, as the written and fixed authority, became the "primary canon" or what some scholars have called the formal canon, while the tradition, or the "functional canon," is the guide or rule possessing fixed and fluid forms that are both oral and written. Although the New Testament, along with the Old Testament, became the *norma normans* (the norm that sets the norm), the historical fact of the matter is that the apostolic tradition is as primitive as the Christian Scripture. The scriptural canon came about in its shape and content as an embodiment of the canonical tradition, and the tradition could only be legitimated by standing in unity with the teaching of Scripture.

Does the above mean that Scripture is subservient to tradition? The very wording of this question is built on a polemical assumption that Scripture and tradition must lie in antithesis to each other. This is a particularly Protestant worry, one that has influenced and shaped post-sixteenth-century theology to a wide and unfortunate extent. Early Christians would have been baffled by framing Scripture and tradition in this way. The ancient fathers themselves taught that the tradition was the epitome of the Christian faith, the very purport of Scripture. A true interpretation of Scripture would always lead one to the tradition. At the same time, all the major creeds and works of theology acknowledged, implicitly or explicitly, the supremacy of the Bible. The early church held Scripture so highly that in times of persecution Christian leaders were held liable for handing over any texts they possessed. As shown in the decisions of the Western Council of Arles (A.D. 314),[20] any clergyman who surrendered the Scripture to the Roman authorities was removed from his position.

In the Protestant mind, the difference between Scripture and tradition is that the revelation of Scripture has ceased completely, and therefore, the Bible is absolutely unique as canon, whereas tradition is not inspired and has not ceased, making it (perhaps) authoritative but not canonical. The problem with this assessment is that it is limited to a narrow view of what the tradition was and is. The church of Jesus Christ has always looked to certain foundational and formative rules or normative expressions of its teaching about God, Christ, salvation, and the world that are found in the patristic tradition. Practically speaking, this tradition has functioned as a canon of Christian belief, especially as the doctrinal and confessional achievement of the fourth and fifth centuries, operating as the historico-theological precedent for all subsequent formulation. Nothing about the patristic process of canonization should be perceived as a threat to the unique place of Scripture's authority. Historical analyses of the ancient Christian concepts of canon show that the canonization of Scripture occurred within the context of canonical tradition and that both emerged out of the life of the patristic church. Both occurred by the enabling of the Holy Spirit, who nurtured and preserved the church. In this regard, let me cite the Montreal Statement one more time: "We exist as Christians by the Tradition of the gospel (the *paradosis* of the *kerygma*) testified in Scripture, transmitted in and by the church through the power of the Holy Spirit."[21] Evangelicals need to hear that not only Scripture but also the tradition was superintended by the work of God's Spirit. God's sovereign purposes were at work in the formation and preservation of the church's structures of belief. Believers are thereby called on to receive this gift as an indelible part of their earthly pilgrimage.

20. *Canon* 14 (13).
21. Rodger and Vischer, *Fourth World Conference on Faith and Order*, 52.

Locating the First "Canon"

The language and concept of canon preceded Christianity's use of it. Without delving into the subject in any depth, we may observe that the term *canon* had a variety of usages in classical antiquity. Literally, the word meant a plumb line or a stick for making measurements. The figurative meaning was more common. A canon was a model or principle by which all other things were judged. Thus, the canon became the norm in a Platonic sense, whether as the perfect form (e.g., the sculpture of the spearman Polycletus, which was the canonical form for the human body)[22] or as an infallible criterion (e.g., principles of logic by which one is able to know what is true or false).[23] It is with the ancient Greek usage in mind that *canon* first appears within a Christian context. In Galatians 6:15, the apostle Paul closes his letter to the Galatians by reminding them that when it comes to the cross of Christ, neither circumcision nor uncircumcision counts for anything. What matters is how Jews and Gentiles can be made a "new creation" according to the redemption that comes through Christ. Rather than measuring oneself by the law of circumcision, Paul says, peace and mercy are upon those who follow "this canon."[24] The mention of canon here has nothing to do with a list of authoritative texts; rather, it refers to a standard or rule of belief and living grounded in the redemptive death of Christ. An earlier reference to this same canon may be alluded to in chapter 2 when Paul complains about those Jews at Antioch who separated themselves from the Gentiles and thus were not acting in line "with the truth of the gospel" (Gal. 2:14).

While this may be the only time Paul actually speaks of a canon, he makes insinuations elsewhere of an existing standard of faith that correlates with his message of the Christian faith. Best known is Paul's outlined version of the tradition in 1 Corinthians 15:3–4:

22. Pliny the Elder, *Natural History* 34.8, 55.
23. G. Kittel and G. Friedrich, eds., *Theological Dictionary of the New Testament*, trans. G. W. Bromiley, 10 vols. (Grand Rapids: Eerdmans, 1964–76), 3:597–98. Epicurus is said to have written a book (now lost) titled *The Criterion of the Canon*, in which he used principles of logic to assess points of value, coherence, and so on in an argument.
24. The NIV translates the word *canon* as "rule."

that Christ died for our sins
that he was buried
that he was raised on the third day

Paul says this threefold litany of events happened in accordance
with the ancient prophets and was witnessed by the apostles. This
is not the only record of the Pauline style of presenting the gospel.
In the course of his first journey to Asia Minor with Barnabas,
"the message of salvation" is reported as the execution of Jesus by
the order of Pilate, his body being laid in a tomb, and God rais-
ing him from the dead (Acts 13:26–35). These events happened
in fulfillment of what God promised "our fathers," just as these
were witnessed by those who were with Jesus. Second Timothy
1:13–14 may be an oblique reference to this preaching, though
without describing its content: "What you heard from me, keep
as the pattern of sound teaching, with faith and love in Christ
Jesus. Guard the good deposit that was entrusted to you." This
"pattern of sound teaching" was by no means something Paul
dreamed up on his own recognizance. Paul says that as he received
it (1 Cor. 11:23; 15:3; Gal. 1:18), so the Thessalonians, for their
sanctification, are to follow the pattern of what they "received"
from Paul (1 Thess. 4:1–3). But this pattern was not the only one
in use at the time. The christological hymn of Philippians 2:5–11,
which recounts the incarnation, crucifixion, and exaltation, echoes
a slightly different and probably more common version of the
church's proclamation. Here Paul is utilizing a preexisting hymn
or liturgical fragment that outlines the salient features of the tradition for mnemonic purposes. Peter's evangelical message in Acts
2:22–36; 3:13–22; and 10:39–43 seems to be constructed upon a
similar plan, making the following points: Jesus Christ was killed,
raised from the dead, and exalted as Lord and Judge. Again, this
preaching of Jesus is affirmed by the Hebrew Scriptures and is
the joint witness of the earliest disciples.

In all the above cases, the reader ought to bear in mind that
these are reports about the transmission of the faith *before* it
was rendered into text (i.e., a letter or narrative) and certainly
well before there was any kind of codification of Christian texts.
Although the earliest stages of the apostolic message do not contain a single structure or content, one does find a set of recurring

themes that are based on the revelation of God in Christ as seen
through his incarnate life; his servanthood through his crucifixion, death, and burial; and the remaking of creation through his
resurrection and realized lordship. There was indeed a sense of
canonical teaching, as the above passages show, that had to do
with standard features of the apostles' preaching. There was also
an initial arrangement for devotional and worshiping practices
in the life of the church, as Acts 2:42 implies: "They devoted
themselves to the apostles' teaching and to the fellowship, to the
breaking of bread and to prayer."

Patristic Tradition as Canon

The fathers of the earliest centuries can be considered authors
and exponents of a "founding" tradition, which has been preserved
and continuously elucidated in subsequent ages. Protestants may
insist that tradition is not revelation, yet they might agree that the
early tradition was and is an element of the Spirit's providential
working to define and preserve the church. Even as the Spirit
continues to incorporate new expressions of the church's faith,
hope, and love into the body of Christ, it does so always under
the guidance of Scripture and in "conversation" with the patristic
tradition. We may not be familiar with patristic terminology or
we may object to the fathers' use of Platonist or Stoic categories,
but the patristic tradition became an indelible part of the Christian faith on which all theology, spirituality, and exegesis have
been built. The place of the patristic tradition, as manifested in
the content of its creeds, catechisms, and doctrinal and moral
theology, has functioned and still functions in a canonical way,
theologically and historically. Practically speaking, this tradition has functioned as a canon of Christian belief, especially the
doctrinal and confessional achievement of the fourth and fifth
centuries, operating as the historico-theological precedent for all
subsequent formulation.

To reiterate, this description of the patristic tradition as canonical is not meant to equate patristic authority with that of the
Bible. Any of the ancient church fathers would have been horrified
to find their written legacy placed on a par with Holy Scripture.
Simply put, the tradition is not revelatory in the way that Scripture

is revelatory. Roman Catholics do refer to tradition as revelation ✓
partly to defend the ongoing work of God in the church, but they
also view this revelation as being on a lower plane than Holy
Writ. Vatican II makes this clear enough. But whether one takes
a Protestant or a Roman Catholic view, the tradition birthed in
the patristic era has been given a preferential place for most of
the church's history. Despite the recognition that each period of
church history has made its own distinct contributions and will
continue to do so, the early church was unique for giving Christianity the canons of Scripture and the tradition.

A well-articulated case for the patristic age as a theological
and credal canon can be found in the Congregation for Catholic
Education's "Instruction on the Study of the Fathers of the Church
in the Formation of Priests."[25] During a dinner conversation several years ago with Cardinal Francis George of the archdiocese
of Chicago, I asked why the Roman Catholic students did not
seem well versed in the writings of the early fathers. For a long
time I had assumed that Roman Catholics were familiar with the
early church and Protestants were not. When I began to teach
at Loyola University in Chicago, I discovered that students from
neither communion knew much about them. Cardinal George did
not disagree with my observation and wondered aloud whether
the longstanding emphasis on philosophical training in Catholic
seminaries had caused church historical studies to become more
marginalized than they should have been. He suggested the above
article as a contribution toward correcting the imbalance. Both
Protestants and Roman Catholics would do well to pay it heed.

Its overall thrust is an encouragement for greater integration
of the study of the early fathers into the curricula of seminaries
and departments of theology. Quite rightly, this article observes
that the present condition of the church, in light of its pastoral
mission and the constant emergence of new currents of spirituality, calls for "healthy nourishment and reliable sources . . . of
true wisdom and Christian authenticity that flow from patristic
works." With good reason does the congregation's instruction
contend that patristic thought provides an excellent model for
catechesis, scriptural understanding, shaping of the tradition,
and knowledge about the whole person by which all subsequent

25. Published in *Origins* 19 (1990): 550–61.

centuries may compare their own proclamation and ministry. As Christ-centered and prime examples of a unified, living theology that "matured in contact with the problems of the pastoral ministry,"[26] the early fathers are called "the privileged witnesses of tradition." Regardless of what should be included as part of the church's tradition, "the fathers are always linked with tradition, having been both its protagonists and its witnesses."[27] Historically, it is through them that the scriptural canon was set, that the basic professions of faith (*regulae fidei*) were composed, and that the deposit of faith in response to heresy and contemporary culture was defined, giving rise to, properly speaking, Christian theology. No less, they gave the first reflective responses to Scripture, formulating these responses within the daily pastoral practice of experience and teaching, having authored the first Christian catecheses, commentaries, and sermons.

Formation of the Tradition as Canon (Orthodoxy)

Describing the canonical tradition of the patristic church is like describing a coat of many colors. It has different shades and hues that portray a composite, sometimes contrasting, garment of faith. When identifying the tradition, therefore, we are dealing not only with oral tradition or creeds but also with various embodiments of the patristic church—doctrine, texts, catechisms, confessions—that reveal how that tradition was shaped.[28] In this light, Irenaeus's introduction to the framework of the apostolic preaching in his day is instructive: "This is the drawing up of our faith, the foundation of the building, and the consolidation of a way of life."[29] Unlike the modern way of making distinctions within the theological enterprise, the ancients tended to conflate faith as doctrine and faith as response, that is, doctrine and practice. The tradition as Christian standard comprises both of these. Thus, believers should not imagine that a rehearsal of the church's faith is something only theologians do. The rule of faith is the "stuff" of the Christian life; it is a way of articulating one's

---

26. Ibid., 553.
27. Ibid., 554.
28. Chapter 5 below will provide further discussion and examples of this variety.
29. Irenaeus, *Demonstration of the Apostolic Preaching* 6.

commitment to God that shares in the commitment of the whole church. Canonical faith is the catholic faith.

The foundation of the church's canon of faith, as per Irenaeus, is modeled on the very revelation of God:

> God the Father, uncreated, beyond grasp, invisible, one God the maker of all . . . the Word of God, the Son of God, Christ Jesus our Lord, who was shown forth by the prophets according to the design of their prophecy and according to the manner in which the Father established; and through him [the Son] were made all things entirely. . . . He became a man among men, visible and tangible, in order to abolish death and bring to light life and bring about communion of God and man. And the third is the Holy Spirit, through the prophets prophesied . . . and who in the end of times has been poured forth in a new manner upon humanity over all the earth renewing man to God.

This is what Irenaeus calls the canon (or rule) of faith. More complex than a baptismal formula, the canon of faith is the norm that seals believers in baptism, expressing the actual process of salvation: "Those who are the bearers of the Spirit of God are led to the Word, that is, to the Son; and the Son takes them and presents them to the Father, and the Father confers incorrupt-ibility."[30] As God sent his Son, who bequeathed the Holy Spirit to all believers, so we return to God, borne by the Spirit according to the gift of the Son.

Irenaeus also speaks of the canon of truth in several instances throughout an anti-Gnostic work titled *Against Heresies* (c. 178). Here he confronts Gnostic ways of construing the written Gospels by separating the Creator God from the Father of our Lord Jesus Christ as another, drawing the conclusion that Christ represented not God the Creator but another God who is the means of our salvation. The upshot of this view is to see the world and Christ's redemption as having no link with each other and to make salva-tion a denial or escape from creation. To this Irenaeus replies, "The disciple of the Lord, therefore, wanting to put an end to all such teaching" should adhere to the "canon of truth in the church" (III.11, 1). The beginning line of the "canon" is cited: "that there is one Almighty God, who made all things by His Word (Christ),

30. Ibid., 7.

both visible and invisible." This shows, Irenaeus says, "that by the Word, through whom God made the creation, He also bestowed salvation on mankind included in the creation." This is the very point of John 1: "In the beginning was the Word, and the Word was with God, and the Word was God. He was with God in the beginning. Through him all things were made; without him nothing was made that has been made" (vv. 1–3). One may read the words of the gospel or consult the "canon" for the truths of the Christian church, which are called the first principles of the gospel (III.11, 7).

A slightly later contemporary of Irenaeus, Tertullian of Carthage, is also familiar with a concise and summary version of the rule of faith as conveyed in North Africa. His three recitals of the rule have been much discussed by scholars.[31] But Tertullian also describes the rule in terms of the tradition at large, expressed in Scripture and in catechetical summaries of the faith. After mentioning the harmony of truth expressed in the four Gospels, he writes:

> These all start with the same rule of the faith, so far as relates to the only one God the Creator and His Christ, how he was born of a virgin, and came as a fulfillment of the law and the prophets. Never mind if there does occur some variation in the order of the narratives, provided that they be in agreement in the essential details.[32]

Those elements that the church believed (*fides quae creditur*) are discovered in the rule of faith, which was a standard for the faith in the sense that it was a distillation of the tradition. It stood for the apostolic faith itself just as it represented the message of Scripture. This is borne out by Tertullian's reference to the rule as the "law of faith" and how he defines an apostate as one who has "lapsed from the Rule of faith."[33] In effect, the rule was a product of and at the same time represented the Christian teaching in its totality. The tradition was most aptly framed in the words of the local rule, a view that continued well into the fourth century. A letter

---

31. E.g., L. William Countryman, "Tertullian and the *Regula Fidei*," *Second Century* 2 (1982): 221–26; and B. Hägglund, "Die Bedeutung der 'regula fidei' als Grundlage theologischer Aussagen," *Studia Theologia* 12 (1958): 1–41.

32. Tertullian, *Against Marcion* IV.2.1.

33. Tertullian, *On the Veiling of Virgins* 1; and idem, *On the Prescription of Heretics* 3.

from the council of Arles in Gaul (A.D. 314) to Sylvester, bishop of Rome, warns about the unstable minds of certain persons who "spit out the present authority, the tradition and the rule of truth of our God."[34] Christians in southern France naturally assumed that the Christians in Rome would know of and also embrace the authority of "the tradition and the rule of truth."

The basic content of the rule is similarly found fifty years after Irenaeus in the works of Hippolytus and Novatian, both clergy in the mid-third-century Roman Church. The *Apostolic Tradition,* ascribed to Hippolytus, usually figures in representative catechisms of early Christian texts.[35] Novatian's *On the Trinity* is lesser known but no less important for establishing the baseline of the tradition of the period. The opening line of the text begins, "The Rule of truth requires that we should first of all things believe on God the Father" and then proceeds to outline the meaning of the Father as omnipotent and Creator (chaps. 1–8), the Son as fully God who appeared to the prophets and is the sole redeemer of humanity (chaps. 9–28), and the Holy Spirit "promised to the church" (chap. 29). One also sees the concept and articulation of the canon of faith expressed in Origen's *On First Principles.* This production, in four books, is among the earliest known attempts to offer a unifying presentation of Christian theology, including God as Father, the Son as "second" to the Father, the Spirit as "third," the creation and destruction of the world, the soul, principalities and powers, and the doctrine of Scripture, "composed through the Spirit of God." All these points, on which Origen elaborates, are part of the "definite line and unmistakable rule" laid down by the church.[36] Such teaching is regarded as the "apostolic teaching," which ought to be believed by all Christians.

The Nicaeanum

Turning to the developments of the fourth and early fifth centuries, we see the rise of statements of faith that represent the activity

34. *Concilia Galliae A. 314–A. 506,* in *Corpus Christianorum, Series Latina,* vol. 148, ed. C. Munier (Turnholt: Brepols, 1963), 4.

35. W. A. Jurgens, *The Faith of the Early Fathers,* vol. 1 (Minneapolis: Liturgical Press, 1970), selection 394a.

36. Origen, *On First Principles* 2.

of the early church more universally than the varied instances of the rule of faith. In fact, the fourth century is a turning point in the patristic period, for without its contributions, the patristic church would not have come to be regarded as canonical. With the Nicene Creed and the events of the years that followed, a more permanent structure of expressing the tradition came to pass and became the primary source of authority for all later ages of the church.

Just like the corpus of Scripture, the normative status of the patristic tradition represented in the Nicene faith was not a foregone conclusion in its earliest stages. The widespread use of the rule of faith notwithstanding, there was no consensus in the beginning of the fourth century about the following: (1) How divine is Jesus Christ (is he God just like the Father is God)? (2) How is a trinitarian understanding of God compatible with the oneness of God? (3) How does Christ's divinity relate to his humanity and vice versa, assuming the full reality of both? Arriving at a resolution for these three major issues, at least confessionally, was the burden of the fourth- and fifth-century church.

We must bear in mind that the Nicene Creed was drafted at a time (A.D. 325) when theological debate over these three issues, especially the first two, was still in its infancy. Although the creed became the chief symbol of the later patristic period, the promulgation of the creed had minimal immediate effect on the theological landscape. At most, the creed served to heighten awareness of the issues that were at stake, but for the next quarter century or so it did little else on a constructive level. The reasons for this are not hard to see. In the early fourth century, precise definitions of important theological terms such as *person* or *substance* and whether the Greek term meant the same thing as the Latin term were yet to find general acceptance.[37] Equally problematic was that there was no agreement about which Bible passages were speaking about the Son's divinity and which were about the Son's humanity. When Jesus declared his dread of the "cup" before him (Matt. 26:37–39) or displayed ignorance about the time of his second coming (Mark 13:32), were these experiences applicable to his human nature?

37. For the Greeks, the word *hypostasis* could be translated in Latin as "substance" or "person." Most Easterners preferred to speak of the Trinity as three *hypostases*, which seemed to Westerners that they were saying that God is three substances, that is, three Gods.

And if so, what did this mean for his divine self? The very notion that God in Christ could really undergo suffering of any kind had rarely been addressed, and different answers abounded. Not until the time Augustine was completing his important work *On the Trinity* in 420 was there some consistency in dealing with such problems.

Regarding the evolution of a Christian doctrine of the Trinity, we cannot assume that the Nicene resolution was somehow built into the understanding of previous centuries. Doctrine did not simply unfold as if the later developments were already present within the early stages. There is no doubt that the second-century way of thinking about the Father and the Son was in terms of ranking: the Son was "second" to the Father; the Father was invisible God while the Son was visible God; the Father was eternal, but the Son emerged or was "begotten" from the Father at some point. Most bishops in the early fourth century took a similar view, since it preserved real distinctions within God. The Son was truly the Son, not the Father; the Son was "begotten" (John 1:14, 18; 3:16), whereas the Father was unbegotten and therefore different from the Son. Those who refused to subordinate the Son to the Father preferred to stress not God's threeness but his oneness. Often called Monarchians for the sole governing of one God, they stressed the unity of the Father and the Son to the degree that the only difference between the two was their names. Sometimes God appeared in history as the Father, and at other times he appeared as the Son, but he was always the same God. In this line of thought, the Son is just as divine as the Father because there is no essential difference between them.

Therefore, when the Nicene Creed declared that the Son is "of the same substance" (*homoousios*) as the Father, to drive home the full divinity of the Son, it sounded strange to many bishops present. Worse than the fact that the term never appears in the Bible (most confessional language prior to that time was taken from the Bible) was that it could easily be given a Monarchian interpretation. Suspicions were aroused because strong supporters of the creed were Eustathius of Antioch and Marcellus of Ancyra, known advocates of a Monarchian-type of view about God. While the Nicene Creed did rule out the kind of subordinationism associated with Arius and his supporters, it failed to articulate

how God is really a Trinity and therefore failed to distance itself
from Monarchianism. In the end, the Nicene Creed did not create the doctrinal unanimity its proponents had intended. It also
said nothing about the relation of the Holy Spirit to the Father
and the Son. For the next thirty years, councils continued to con-
vene and propose other creeds with startling rapidity. Scholars of
early Christianity have designated this period the era of creeds
and councils. During this time, the Nicene Creed was merely one
option among many.

By the 360s, the introduction of one creed after another had
done little to achieve doctrinal harmony and had spent itself.[38] Just
as important was the process of interpretation and reinterpretation
that the Nicene Creed had been undergoing. An often-overlooked
synod that met in Alexandria in 362 played an important role in
the new reception of the Nicene Creed.[39] From the small amount
of documentation that survives from this council, we know that
it sent a conciliar letter to the church in Antioch acknowledging that the Holy Spirit is one God with the Father and the Son,
because he is "proper to and inseparable from the essence of the
Father and the Son."[40] Moreover, the council declared that the
Nicene faith and its same-substance language (*homoousios*) was
compatible with an emphasis on God as three (three *hypostases*).
This was a critical recognition on the part of this council, one
that was elaborated on and refined in the theological writings of
Gregory of Nazianzus and Gregory of Nyssa. Under their pens,
Nicene theology became completely dissociated from the tinge
of Monarchianism that had hounded the Nicene Creed from its
inception.[41] In addition, attention was drawn to the complete
divinity of the Holy Spirit as being of one substance with the
Father and the Son.[42] What these interpretations offered was a

38. For the ecclesiastical and political side of how the Nicene Creed rose to dominance,
see D. H. Williams, *Ambrose of Milan and the End of the Nicene-Arian Conflicts* (Oxford:
Oxford University Press, 1995), chap. 1.

39. A. De Halleux, "La Réception du Symbole Oecuménique, de Nicée à Chalcédoine,"
Ephemerides Theologicae Lovaniensis 61 (1985): 11–12.

40. Tomus 5, in *The Nicene and Post-Nicene Fathers*, 2nd series, vol. 4, ed. P. Schaff
and H. Wace (Grand Rapids: Eerdmans, 1987), 484.

41. For this point, I am indebted to Michel Barnes, "The Fourth Century as Trinitarian Canon," in *Christian Origins: Theology, Rhetoric, and Community*, ed. L. Ayres and
G. Jones, 47–67 (London: Routledge, 1998).

42. Gregory of Nazianzus, *Oration* 31.9–10.

way of emphasizing God's threeness without subordinating the Son, and preserving God's oneness without making Father, Son, and Spirit a numerical identity. The council in 362 and others not mentioned here, as well as the theology of the Cappadocians, are symptomatic of a new turn in the perception of the Nicene faith. One can trace this reception across the lines of Eastern and Western theologians.

By the time of the Council of Constantinople in 381, the Nicene Creed had become pivotal in the preservation of Christian faithfulness.[43] Unfortunately, minutes from the Council of Constantinople were not made or do not survive, and apart from a few interchurch decisions (called "canons"), no record of a creed from the council exists. We know, however, from a conciliar letter to the emperor Theodosius that the council was intent on affirming Nicaea and decided to condemn heresies that had arisen against it. The records preserved at the Council of Chalcedon seventy years later reveal that the Nicene Creed figured into the council's proceedings but in a slightly reinterpreted form, now known as the Nicene-Constantinopolitan Creed.

> I believe in one God, the Father Almighty, Maker of heaven and earth, and of all things visible and invisible.
>
> And in one Lord Jesus Christ, the only-begotten Son of God, begotten of the Father before all worlds; God of God, Light of Light, very God of very God; begotten, not made, being of one substance with the Father; by whom all things were made.
>
> Who, for us men for our salvation, came down from heaven, and was incarnate by the Holy Spirit of the virgin Mary, and was made man; and was crucified also for us under Pontius Pilate; He suffered and was buried; and the third day He rose again, according to the Scriptures; and ascended into heaven, and sits on the right hand of the Father; and He shall come again, with glory, to judge the living and the dead; whose kingdom shall have no end.

43. The Nicene Creed: We believe in one God, the Father, almighty, maker of all things visible and invisible; and in one Lord Jesus Christ, the son of God, begotten from the Father, only-begotten, that is, from the substance of the Father, God from God, light from light, true God from true God, begotten not made, of one substance from the Father, through Whom all things came into being, things in heaven and things on earth, who because of us men and because of our salvation came down and became incarnate, becoming man, suffered and rose again on the third day, ascended to the heavens, will come to judge the living and the dead; and in the Holy Spirit.

And I believe in the Holy Ghost, the Lord and Giver of Life; who proceeds from the Father and the Son; who with the Father and the Son together is worshipped and glorified; who spoke by the prophets.

And I believe in one holy catholic and apostolic Church. I acknowledge one baptism for the remission of sins; and I look for the resurrection of the dead, and the life of the world to come. Amen.

It has been much debated whether this creed is an expansion of the Nicene Creed or comes from another source because the phrase "from the substance of the Father, God from God" is missing, along with some other terms.[44] It also contains the phrase "from the Father and the Son" in regard to the Holy Spirit's procession, probably a later Western inclusion, which is still contested by Eastern Orthodoxy as an unwarranted addition to Nicene theology. Another difference is that this creed is more thoroughly trinitarian than the Nicene; each member of the Trinity is described in relation to the other members. The creed of 325 says less about the Father and only mentions the Holy Spirit with no description at all, since the focus of the time was fixed on how the Son is no less divine than the Father. Nevertheless, in one of the big quirks of church history, this Constantinopolitan Creed was most often identified as the Nicene Creed until the present day, largely because it was appointed in the second half of the fifth century to be sung in the liturgy of the Eastern church and about a century later regularly appeared in the baptismal and eucharistic services in the West.

The next two ecumenical councils, Ephesus (431) and Chalcedon (451), defined the true faith according to the Nicene Creed (i.e., the Nicene-Constantinopolitan Creed). Canon 7 issued at Ephesus reveals that these Christian leaders agreed that no new creed should be brought forward or composed "besides that which was settled by the holy fathers who assembled at Nicea, with the Holy Spirit."[45] It

44. "God from God" may have been a redundancy, but the reason for dropping "from the substance of the Father," Hanson surmises, is that it had material or corporeal suggestions. R. P. C. Hanson, "The Achievement of Orthodoxy in the Fourth Century AD," in *The Making of Orthodoxy: Essays in Honour of Henry Chadwick*, ed. R. Williams (Cambridge: Cambridge University Press, 1989), 154.

45. It may surprise evangelicals who claim the ecumenical councils as doctrinal authorities to learn that the Council of Ephesus made the title "Theotokos" ("God-bearer") official for the virgin Mary, thus stimulating and deepening Marian devotion in both East and West. Even so, the original impetus behind "Theotokos" was not Mary but the full divinity of the One born to her.

is evident that Nicaea and the revised creed associated with it had attained a normative status, a status that was apparent to the fathers at Chalcedon. The preface to the creed of Chalcedon reads:

> This then we have done, having, by mutual agreement, driven away the doctrines of error, and having renewed the unerring faith of the Fathers, proclaiming to all the creed of the 318 [bishops] and endorsing as our own the Fathers who received this godly document, namely the 150 [bishops], who later met together in great Constantinople and set their seal to the same faith.
>
> We decree, therefore . . . that the exposition of the orthodox and irreproachable faith set forth by the 318 holy and blessed Fathers who met at Nicaea . . . retain its place of honor, and also that definition of the 150 holy Fathers at Constantinople, for the removal of the heresies then recently sprung up, and for the confirmation of our same Catholic and Apostolic faith, continue still in force.[46]

There follows the citation of the Nicene (325) and Nicene-Constantinopolitan creeds, to which is then added a qualification about the Son's incarnation that stresses the perfection and inviolability of his divinity and humanity as two separate natures in one person. Thus, the Chalcedonian Creed is, like the one presumably from Constantinople (381), an expansion of the Nicene formula, ensuring orthodox teaching regarding the dual nature of the God-man, Jesus Christ. Even so, the "confirmation of our same Catholic and Apostolic faith" was the joining of the Nicene and Constantinopolitan creeds. It is noteworthy that the decree of Chalcedon uses the singular, not the plural, to refer to both statements: "The wise and saving creed."[47]

In sum, these creeds function "canonically" when they communicate not only the literal terms of the creeds themselves but also the interpretation that lifted these creeds from among their conciliar peers and made them normative.[48] As with the reception of Nicaea, it was just as important to configure the meaning of the creed as it was to recount its words. Reminiscent of the fixed fluidity of the rule of faith of earlier centuries, the Chris-

---

46. Cited in J. Stevenson and W. H. C. Frend, eds., *Creeds, Councils, and Controversies: Documents Illustrating the History of the Church AD 337–461* (London: SPCK, 1989), 350.

47. Jaroslav Pelikan, *Credo: Historical and Theological Guide to Creeds and Confessions of Faith in the Christian Tradition* (New Haven: Yale University Press, 2003), 14.

48. Barnes, "Fourth Century as Trinitarian Canon," 62.

tian leaders at Alexandria, Constantinople, and Chalcedon did not believe that the way of doctrinal faithfulness lay in the literal reproduction of the Nicene Creed.[49] In fact, it took the theological developments of a "neo-Nicene" interpretation of the creed over the course of a century for the creed to return to general acceptance and circulation within the churches.

Beyond Chalcedon, future church councils looked to the Nicene Creed as the beginning point for establishing orthodoxy. No matter how many more ecumenical councils one accepts, whether a total of seven with the Eastern Orthodox[50] or twenty-one with Roman Catholicism,[51] or whether other important but not ecumenical councils figure as authoritative sources for doctrine,[52] none of these shares the same foundational character as the patristic creeds of the fourth and fifth centuries. The so-called fifth ecumenical council (Constantinople II) "set its seal to the Creed which was put forth by the 318 fathers [Nicene] and again piously confirmed by the 150 [Constantinople, 381] which also other holy synods received and ratified." A similar affirmation was made by the sixth and seventh ecumenical councils. The seventh, or the Council of Nicaea II, made it clear that the Nicene Creed was preeminent among the later ecumenical creeds. Unto the present day then, the Nicene Creed is the statement par excellence of what the Christian church believes, as one finds in the liturgies of Roman Catholicism, Anglicanism, Eastern Orthodoxy, and various Protestant orders of service. Along with the Apostles' Creed, the Nicene Creed (in its original and liturgical forms) has been the heart of ecumenical confessionalism and is the basis on which nearly all Christian communions can agree.

Precedents for Theological Canonicity

Making appeal to the patristic faith as norm or canon is admittedly a retrospective observation. By its very nature, a canon is

49. De Halleux, "La Réception," 25.

50. In addition to the first four, Constantinople (553), Constantinople (680), and Nicaea (787) are designated "ecumenical" because they were supposedly councils of the undivided church. These seven stand as the formal deposit of normative teaching for Eastern Orthodoxy.

51. C. J. Hefele, *A History of the Christian Councils* (Edinburgh: T & T Clark, 1894), 63–64.

52. E.g., Serdica (342/3), Carthage (397), and Toledo (400).

regarded as canonical only as its contents are consistently received and generally accepted as unique sources of authority. This is what lay behind the definition of the catholic faith given by Vincent of Lérins, basing it on the rules of universality, antiquity, and general consent.[53] Similar to the history of the Nicene Creed is the reception of the broader patristic tradition. Recognition of its authority was a reflexive and *post hoc* series of events that came to characterize the orthodox identity of the Christian church.

Lest one still imagines that the functional canonicity of the patristic theological legacy is an idiosyncratic category of my own making, one should consider the following stages briefly summarized.

First, specific terminology in reference to the patristic faith as "norm" or "canon" is not found in Luther and Melanchthon, yet the concept is indigenous to their assumptions about church history. By advocating the sufficiency of Scripture, Luther never intended to reject the sources that the church had held and used for the past fifteen hundred years. Nor did he share the same idea about the institutional church's "fall" with the Anabaptists. His attitude toward the teaching established by the early church revealed a critical but constructive view of the church's history. As Luther worked toward constructing an understanding of church history, he continued to value the importance of the early creeds and writings of the fathers as vehicles for protecting the church from error. Not that the early period of the church provided him with an ideal age to which one must return. It operated rather like that of the Old Testament patriarchs for the church: that of revealing a permanent pattern that modeled faithfulness for all future believers.

It was especially important when instructing new believers to expose them to the church's foundational teaching. In a sermon Luther preached on the catechism in 1528, he stated concerning the Apostles' Creed, "This teaching [the Apostles' Creed] is different from that of the commandments [the Ten Commandments]. The commandments teach what we should do, but the Creed teaches what we have received from God. The Creed, therefore, gives you what you need. This is the Christian faith."[54] The same attitude

---

53. Vincent of Lérins, *Commonitorium* I.2, 6.

54. From "Sermons on the Creed," in *Martin Luther: Selections from His Writings*, ed. J. Dillenberger (Garden City, N.Y.: Doubleday, 1961), 214.

is espoused with regard to the Nicene Creed, to which believers are urged to adhere as the best explanation of the doctrine of the Trinity. Nicaea was an important conciliar moment in church history not only because it demonstrated that the primacy of Rome had not existed in the early church but also because it set forth a theological measuring stick. In regard to the four great councils (Nicaea, Constantinople, Ephesus, and Chalcedon) and their creeds, Luther asserted that they established no new articles of faith but merely defended what had been given by the Holy Spirit to the apostles at Pentecost.[55]

Until the end of his life, Luther maintained that a reform of the church should be accomplished by convening a general council. Authority for the proposed council ought to be grounded, he said, in the authority of the four great councils, Nicaea (325), Constantinople (381), Ephesus (431), and Chalcedon (451), which established the norm for Christian doctrine. Because the message of these creeds was wholly commensurate with the message of the gospel as found in Scripture, all subsequent conciliar decisions must be judged according to their doctrinal standards.[56] Such a view marked the perspective of the Protestant Reformation generally, as in Melanchthon, who cited the early fathers and creeds throughout the Augsburg Confession as authorities for determining the true Christian faith from the false. The first article of faith states, "The churches among us teach with complete unanimity that the decree of the Council of Nicaea concerning the unity of the divine essence and concerning the three persons is true and is to be believed without any doubt."[57] Veritably hundreds of citations from the ancient fathers are cited in confirmation of the newly emerging Lutheran theology.

In the early Reformed tradition, Calvin stated that the language of consubstantiality in the Nicene Creed was "simply expounding the real meaning of Scripture," being the work of the Holy Spirit.[58]

55. Martin Luther, "On the Councils and the Church," in *Luther's Works*, ed. T. G. Tapert and H. T. Lehmann (St. Louis: Concordia, 1955), 50.551, 607.

56. Ibid., 41.121–22. In *The Three Symbols or Creeds of the Christian Faith* (1538), Luther published his own edited versions of the Apostles' Creed and Athanasian Creed as well as the *Te Deum* (a hymnic confession), to which the Nicene Creed was appended.

57. R. Kolb and T. Wengert, eds., *The Book of Concord* (Minneapolis: Fortress, 2000), 37.

58. John Calvin, *Institutes of the Christian Religion*, ed. J. T. McNeill, trans. F. L. Battles (Philadelphia: Westminster, 1960), IV.viii.16.

Although complete primacy was given to Scripture in all matters of doctrine and life, Calvin defended the patristic position that nonscriptural terms had to be used in order to define a scriptural understanding of God.[59] All the major fathers confirmed the orthodox doctrine of the Trinity, as did the ancient councils (Nicaea, Constantinople, Ephesus, and Chalcedon), of which Calvin says, "I venerate from my heart and desire that they be honored by all."[60] As his *Reply to Cardinal Sadoleto* (1539) shows, Calvin was convinced that the Reformation was in line with the doctrines of the early church. The true church that the apostles instituted is commensurate with the ancient form of the church, exhibited by the writings of Chrysostom and Basil, among the Greek writers, and Cyprian, Ambrose, and Augustine and is "embodied in our religion."

Second, the Reformers drew their knowledge of patristic church history largely from medieval collections of canon law and anthologies of excerpted patristic texts, which, before the fifteenth century, were the primary means by which readers were exposed to texts of the early fathers.[61] The most influential collection was the massive twelfth-century *Harmony of Discordant Canons*, later known as the *Decree of Gratian*. It taught with absolute certainty that the "four venerable synods, before all others, shelter the whole of the faith, like the four Gospels or the like-numbered rivers of Paradise. . . . These four chief synods proclaim most fully the doctrine of the faith."[62] Other subsequent councils were recognized, but they were subject to the authority of these four.[63] Overall, the *Decree* presents thousands of citations and allusions to the ancient fathers, although

59. Ibid., I.xiii.3.
60. The four councils are distinguished from all subsequent councils since only the four contain nothing but "the pure and genuine exposition of Scripture," which the holy fathers applied with spiritual prudence against the enemies of the faith (ibid., IV.ix.8).
61. Not until the early sixteenth century were actual editions of the most important fathers available. See Irena Backus, "The Early Church in the Renaissance and Reformation," in *Early Christianity: Origins and Evolution to A.D. 600*, ed. I. Hazlett, 291–303 (Nashville: Abingdon, 1991).
62. *Gratian: The Treatise on Laws (Decretum DD 1–20) with the Ordinary Gloss*, trans. A. Thompson and J. Gordley (Washington, D.C.: Catholic University of America Press, 1993), pars I, dist. XV.1.
63. Distinction XVI.8 professes eight ecumenical councils to be "held worthy of equal honor and veneration." This contradicts the above resolution, though such contradictions are in keeping with the decree's presentation of discordant historical data.

they are dispersed among conciliar decisions, pontifical letters, and decrees, making it difficult to discern patristic from later historical material. Nevertheless, the *Decree* functioned for the rest of the Middle Ages and the Reformation as the primary source treasury for encountering select passages from the early fathers.

Another major sourcebook of patristic testimonia was found in *Glossa Ordinaria* (also called *The Gloss*), itself a series of patristic quotations on the Bible from the ninth century. The ancient comments were originally arranged in the margins of each page of the Bible, but eventually the comments were published in a separate volume. *The Gloss* was heavily utilized by Thomas Aquinas in his thirteenth-century commentary on the four Gospels called *Catena Aurea* (*The Golden Chain*),[64] in which he fashioned a continuous chain of passages compiled entirely from the writings of the early fathers. For his *catenae* on Matthew, Aquinas made almost exclusive use of the Latin fathers, with the notable exception of the Greek writers, John Chrysostom, and occasional citations from Gregory of Nyssa and Gregory of Nazianzus.

Third, the medieval canonical collections were themselves based on select Latin proponents of late patristic opinion. Second only to Augustine's works were the writings of Gregory of Rome ("the Great"), whose bishopric is placed by church historians at either the end of the patristic period or the beginning of the medieval period. In one of his many letters that are preserved, he declared, "I receive and revere as the four books of the gospel so also the four councils," that is, the Nicene, Constantinopolitan, Ephesus, and Chalcedonian, "since on them, as on a four-square stone, rises the structure of the holy faith."[65] Gregory admits he also accepts other later councils, but it is upon the four first councils, "having been constituted by universal consent," that the norms for Christian faith and life reside. We may regard Gregory's arguments as "traditional," for he is drawing on previous patristic writers, not only for the fourfold view of councils but even for his analogies of fourfold as a sacrosanct number because of the four Gospels.

---

64. John Henry Newman, ed. and trans., *Catenae Aurea: Commentary on the Four Gospels* (Oxford: J. H. Parker, 1841), recently reprinted with an introduction by A. Nichols (London: Saint Austin Press, 1999). Thomas completed his first and most substantial volume on Matthew's Gospel by 1264, dedicated to Pope Urban IV.

65. Gregory of Rome, *Epistle* 25.

Gregory shared the structure of authority that Vincent of Lérins had outlined a century earlier. Orthodox Christianity could be proven in two ways: "first, by the authority of the divine canon (the Bible), and the other by the tradition of the catholic church." The authority of the first outweighed the authority of the second, for Vincent claims that the canon (of Scripture) suffices alone on any matter. But he acknowledged that the Bible cannot function in isolation from the early church's tradition lest it fall prey to faulty interpretations. A rule of faith or norm for interpretation is essential if orthodox faith is to be achieved. "It is therefore necessary that the interpretation of divine Scripture should be ruled according to the one standard of the church's belief, especially in those articles on which the foundations of all catholic doctrine rest."[66]

Because the patristic and medieval ages always sought classical wisdom as prerequisites for establishing authority, we should expect the kind of thought expressed above about the patristic past. However, it would be a mistake to portray the late antique mind as not having self awareness about what it was doing and why. Preservation of ancient *auctoritates* (authorities) did have its limits. Many manuscripts deemed carriers of views unfaithful to the tradition were either corrected (a nightmare for text historians!) or conveniently "lost." Clearly, for the Lutheran, the Reformed, some Anabaptist Reformers, and virtually all the medieval writers, the patristic age acted as the norm of the apostolic and catholic faith. It was, in effect, the theological canon of the church. The shape of the major doctrines finally achieved in the fourth and fifth centuries had become a permanent fixture of the Christian faith. None of this meant that future theological exploration and reflections were to be discouraged. Councils continued to meet after Chalcedon. Important doctrinal gains were made in the millennium following the patristic age, gains not only of deeper insight into already established doctrinal truths (e.g., Bonaventure's explication of Christ's redemptive suffering) but also of reconfiguring how one thinks of these truths (e.g., Aquinas's construal of the Trinity or Anselm's theory of the God-man's incarnation). Always integral to such growth was that it

---

66. Gregory of Rome, *Commonitorium* I.29, 76. This part is really the end of the second book of the *Commonitorium*, the first part being lost.

was built directly on the solutions of the patristic achievement, which had forever etched a trinitarian character and its implications into Christian theology and worship.

How Not to Use the Early Fathers

Admittedly, arguing for the patristic tradition as theologically normative can be pushed to extremes. The early fathers have been idealized so that everything they said provides good guidance for today's church. One can resort to the patristic legacy as a "golden age" that Christians should recall from the past, as if invoking it ushers into the present a sort of historical power. An exceptional find in the Egyptian desert some years ago was a papyrus fragment that contained a portion of the text of the Nicene-Constantinopolitan Creed (A.D. 381). The fragmentary portion dates from the later fifth century, and scholars think it may have been used as a kind of amulet.[67] Evidently, the wearer of this credal formula thought that the creed possessed power such that it could invite God's blessing or ward off evil spirits and misfortune!

This chapter is not advocating the patristic legacy as if it were an ecclesiastical charm bracelet, nor should it be interpreted to mean that a reclamation of all or any one aspect of the ancient tradition will solve all the denominational splits and doctrinal muddles that beset contemporary Christianity. As stated in the preface, the notion of *ressourcement* is not about romantically reappropriating the early fathers as if they hold all the answers for contemporary Christians and churches. The patristic tradition was not and is not infallible. None of the creeds that originated from that age is inerrant. Even the staunchest defender of the contemporary relevance of patristic resources will admit that not everything the patristic fathers taught is true or even valuable.

While the patristic faith predates the great church schisms of 1054 and later, it also is a mistake to depict the ancient faith as presenting a uniform expression of doctrine that bears witness to a single faith. Some recent Protestant writers, who have a newfound

---

67. "Fragment of the Niceno-Constantinopolitan Creed," in *New Documents Illustrating Early Christianity,* ed. G. H. R. Horsley (Macquarie: The Ancient History Documentary Research Centre, 1981), 103–4.

zeal for appropriating the early fathers in the face of theological modernity, have been inclined toward idealistic presentations of them and their value for us today. On the one hand, to claim the authority of the patristic consensual tradition may easily be interpreted in a crude metaphysical sense unless we understand that the church's historic witnesses must always be heard within the rough and tumble world of interchurch polemics, uncertainty, and no one agreed-upon method of biblical exegesis. The early church was truly engaged in a search—sometimes haphazardly—for a Christian doctrine of God rather than slowly unveiling what it knew implicitly all along. When it comes to acknowledging the foundational creeds, we are faced with viewing them not merely as doctrinal touchstones but as diachronic statements of faith whose theological and polemical contexts are just as important as the words themselves.

We may agree with certain Protestant theologians who say that whatever authoritative status we attribute to the great conciliar creeds, particularly the Nicene Creed, they are not binding on the Christian faith or conscience.[68] In reply, one might say that neither is the Mosaic law, which constitutes a number of the books Christians regard as canonical. The dialogical form in which the major creeds were formulated (the augmentation of the Nicene Creed at Constantinople and Chalcedon) underscores the idea that these statements were *constructions* of how the church addressed its present circumstances by utilizing what it had received. This is why there are so many ecclesiastical creeds in the fourth century and beyond. They were, in effect, milestones of the tradition's argument with itself about the nature of orthodoxy as new doctrinal issues were addressed in light of what the church had always believed.

Excursus: The Bible as Canon

With the rise of a biblical canon in the later patristic era, the canon of the church's tradition was not eclipsed or outmoded. It is misguided to assert that the early tradition receded as the

68. Most recently, Everett Ferguson made this point in a paper about how a free churchman should appraise and receive the patristic legacy. See Everett Ferguson, "Article Review," *Scottish Journal of Theology* 55 (2002): 104.

canonization of Scripture proceeded. Changes in the role of the rule of faith took place after the third century, but this was not because of an ascending scriptural canon.

What is remarkable about the historic emphasis on the canon of the Bible is that the terminology of "canon" or "rule" is virtually never used for sacred books until the later fourth century, and even then there is only sparse mention. The fact that there was very little interest on the part of the patristic church to formulate a canonical list of books testifies to its lack of importance. The comment by F. F. Bruce that the earliest Christians did not trouble themselves about the criteria of canonicity of texts[69] rings true. Marcion's insistence that only the Pauline Epistles and an expurgated version of Luke's Gospel presented true Christianity is easily overinterpreted to mean that he was propounding a scriptural canon and thereby instigated the early church to do likewise. Despite the prevalent theory that Marcion prompted, at least indirectly, the growth of the biblical canon, we know of no second- or third-century writer who responded to Marcion's considerable theological challenge with a fixed canon of books. In the case of Justin, Irenaeus, Tertullian, Ephrem of Nisibis, and the many others who responded in writing, the Marcionite position was attacked through highlighting the canon of truth or the rule of faith. While it is true that the majority of churches were using the four Gospels, Acts, the Pauline Epistles, and some other epistles as Scripture by the early second century and found Marcion's "Bible" unacceptable, there was nothing like a unity about the extent or parameters of the biblical books. Opposition to Marion, therefore, could not have been in the form of an alternative, "orthodox" canon of texts.

The same generally applies to the patristic approach to Gnosticism. Serapion of Antioch complained that the gospel of Peter was being read (i.e., as Scripture) in the worship services of some churches.[70] The problem was that the text carries manifestly docetic ideas about Christ,[71] ideas that were unacceptable for an orthodox view of Jesus Christ as portrayed in the Gospels. Serapion declared that the ultimate rejection of the heretical gospel was

---

69. Bruce, *Canon of Scripture*, 255.

70. Eusebius, *Ecclesiastical History* VI.12.

71. A "docetic" Christ is one whose physical reality is mitigated or denied. Gnostics were not the only groups to think this way.

not because it was missing from lists of scriptural books but because it violated the traditional faith of the (Antiochene) church. Down the coast in Alexandria, a Christian thinker named Clement (d. 220) faulted the Gnostics with an inability to understand the Bible because they failed to understand the tradition. In his words, the Gnostics needed to explain Scripture according to the "canon of truth" (or the "ecclesiastical rule"), which entailed a proper understanding of the harmony between the Old and New Testaments.[72]

To find the small handful of remarks about the extent of the biblical canon, one has to dig in the known writings of later patristic authors for comment on the subject. Overall, the matter appears to have had limited importance for them, acknowledged in polemical contexts or for instruction in the Christian faith. It is in this context that the famous Muratorian Fragment and Athanasius's Easter letter 39 may be placed. Much has been written about both of these,[73] so let me offer three other less celebrated (but no less important) examples.

Besides (perhaps) the Muratorian Fragment, Eusebius of Caesarea is the earliest source for providing a catalog of biblical books that were accepted in his day. He is acquainted with the term *canon*,[74] but it is not his preferred terminology, likely because there was no one fixed body of biblical books by the late third and early fourth century. His narration is built around which books were the "acknowledged writings," which were disputed, and which were spurious. He was keenly interested to report how illustrious Christian thinkers in the church's history used Scrip-

---

72. Clement, *Stromata* VI.15, 125.

73. The so-called Muratorian canon, a list of books in the New Testament, is found in the Codex Muratorianus, a fragmented seventh- or eighth-century manuscript that also contains confessions of faith, homilies on Scripture, and other theological subjects. The dating of the fragment is problematic, ranging from the late second to the fourth century (see G. M. Hahneman, *The Muratorian Fragment and the Development of the Canon* [Oxford: Clarendon Press, 1992]). Athanasius addressed a letter every year to his congregation in Alexandria at Easter time. Letter 39 was the annual communication for the year 367, according to the internal chronology of the collection. T. D. Barnes, *Athanasius and Constantius: Theology and Politics in the Constantinian Empire* (Cambridge: Harvard University Press, 1993), 189.

74. Eusebius states (*Ecclesiastical History* III.9, 5) that Josephus gave the "number of the canonical writings in the Old Testament" (*Reply to Apion* 1.8). The term *canonical* is Eusebian, not from Josephus. The phrase "canon of the church" is used of Origen's knowledge of the extent of the biblical books (VI.25, 3).

ture and which books they used. For Eusebius, the undisputed biblical books were authoritative because they were "recognized by the churches under heaven" (III.24, 2), and as such, these writings were those "acknowledged" by the churches. Several times Eusebius summarized the books of the Old Testament. Only once did he itemize the writings of the New Testament (III.25, 1–7), explaining that only the four Gospels, Acts, the epistles of Paul, one of Peter, one of John, and perhaps Revelation were among the "acknowledged" texts. It appears that "disputed books" were read in many churches, as were the spurious.

Roughly seventy years later, Augustine enumerated a list of scriptural books accepted in the West in *On Christian Teaching*, a theological handbook for fellow pastors on interpreting the Bible. Typical of patristic authors, Augustine saw the Bible as a completely divine product; every sentence and possible meaning were intended by the Spirit's inspiration. Augustine's attempt to nail down an official list of books is indicative of a situation that lacked a single list. There was no one authoritative version of the Bible. Indeed, readers are told that when it comes to determining the authoritative list of books, they should follow the lead of as many catholic churches as possible. In the case of those books not universally accepted, they should prefer those received by a majority of churches. This did not mean that the collection of Scripture known to him was not canonical. Several times Augustine called Scripture canonical or the canon.[75] What he called the "authoritative Old Testament" contained forty-four books, following the Septuagint version, and is reflected today in the Roman Catholic Bible. There seemed to be less controversy over the boundaries of the "authoritative New Testament," which squares with versions of the Bible today.

Another canonical list is found in a document known as the *Canons of the Constitutions of the Holy Apostles*. This work is a kind of appendix to the larger *Constitutions*, both of which are compilations of different works from different times edited together around the late fourth or early fifth century. In canon 85, the writer provides a complete inventory of the Old and New Testaments, adding to the New Testament *1* and *2 Clement* and eight books of the *Constitutions* (falsely) attributed to Clement.

75. Augustine, *On Christian Teaching* II.24, 26.

Given the antiquity and revered status of *1* and *2 Clement*, it is not surprising that they are mentioned among the biblical books, though the motives of the author are suspicious. Inclusion of the *Constitutions* is completely irregular and represents nothing more than special pleading on the writer's part in order to identify himself with the historic Clement and win acceptance of his work. The fact that such a tactic was tried underlines the lack of fixity that the biblical canon possessed even four centuries after the apostles.

Untidy Canonization

Overall, the process of biblical canonization was much less neat and categorical than modern renditions of the process make it out to be. The reason for this is important precisely because the reasons are difficult to quantify. Determination of the shape and content of the biblical canon, just like the theological canon, occurred as the text was received and consistently affirmed by individual churches. At Baylor University, students in my courses on patristic studies are usually more comfortable if we can pinpoint concrete events that gave rise to the scriptural canon. One can see a certain amount of frustration on their faces as they discover the inadequacy of cause and effect reasons to explain the process. We cannot point simply to the Jewish precedents of the Jewish scholars who met at Jabneh (Jamnia) at the end of the first century and acknowledged the twenty-two books of the Old Testament,[76] or to the negative influence of Marcionism that compelled Christians to create an orthodox canon, or to a church council that decided the issue of the biblical books once and for all.[77] The more mundane truth is that the canonical pro-

76. Whatever credence should be attributed to Jabneh, its purpose seems to have been aimed at providing clarity about only the third part of the Hebrew Bible, the hagiographa.

77. None of the so-called ecumenical or any major council, East or West, treated the matter of biblical canonization. A small council that met in Rome in 382 is thought to have enumerated the canonical books of both testaments in a document known as the Tome of Damasus. Damasus was bishop of Rome and convoked councils of bishops to set church policy throughout Italy, but it is doubtful that the biblical list, which one manuscript also calls the "Decree of Gelasius on Which Books Should and Should Not Be Received," is actually from the proceedings of the council.

cess of tradition and text occurred primarily in the context of the believing community. Canonical "testing" took place within the give and take of church life. James Sanders states the dynamic at work: "The community shaped the text as it moved toward canon and the text or tradition shaped the communities as it found its pilgrimage toward canon."[78] The infrequent references to a normative list of texts suggest that Christian churches were not looking to create a canon but were seeking to hear God's Word in the Scripture readings during worship and ascertain which readings conveyed this Word. Public reading of Scripture is mentioned explicitly by Paul in 1 Timothy 4:13 as an activity intended for the entire church. In the process of liturgically reading in assembly, authoritative weight was accrued by texts that lent to their canonization.[79] Though perhaps more inchoate and unpredictable than we would like, there was, nevertheless, discernment in the process. In this manner, the church, for example, came to reject the gospel of Peter and the gospel of Thomas, whereas it continued to embrace Matthew, Mark, Luke, and John.[80]

---

78. James Sanders, *From Sacred Story to Sacred Text* (Minneapolis: Fortress, 1987), 163.

79. Frank Senn, *Christian Liturgy* (Minneapolis: Fortress, 1997), 70–71.

80. A fuller study on the canonical process will be forthcoming by Craig Allert in this same series.

The Confluence of the Bible, the Tradition, and the Church

For every man alone thinkes he hath got
To be a Phoenix, and that then can bee
None of that kinde, of which he is, but hee.

John Donne, *An Anatomie of the World*

IT MAY COME as a surprise to some readers that for most of church history Scripture and tradition were perceived as generally compatible with each other. The tradition, or the catholic teaching, was the distillation of biblical truth and theoretically always existed in an interrelated harmony with Scripture. In response to the religious leader of a group whose members vaunted themselves as true Christians but who rejected the truly human birth of Christ, Augustine said, "The catholic, which is also the apostolic, doctrine is that our Lord and Savior Jesus Christ is both the Son of God in his divine nature and the Son of David after the flesh. . . . This teaching represents the 'plainest statement in Holy Scripture.'"[1] Like streams coming out of the same spring, the tradition and the Bible, represented by the work of the Holy Spirit in the church, were realized only in the presence of each other. The Bible, no less than the other two, was not to be understood in grand isolation because it had primal authority.

But for the last four centuries or so, the relationship between Scripture and tradition has been a matter of controversy, often posed as one of the major problem areas in Protestant and Roman Catholic relations. One can hardly discuss the rise of the Christian tradition without reference to its authority in comparison to the authority of sacred Scripture. Unfortunately, the moment we turn our focus to Scripture and tradition, especially for many evangelicals, the subject becomes charged with defensiveness. The theological concern goes like this: The Bible is revelation and therefore necessary and binding upon Christian belief and practice, whereas the tradition is human-made and therefore extraneous and nonbinding. The one is canonical and completely authoritative, while the other is noncanonical but has pretensions of such authority. In cruder descriptions, the Bible is from God, while the tradition is of human origination emerging from the church as it was before the Protestant Reformation.

Stress placed on the Bible's authority is often formulated in historical terms of an antithesis between what came before and what came after the Protestant Reformation. Only with the advent of the sixteenth-century Reformation was the Bible restored to its rightful place as the sole authority, distinguished from the various traditional practices of the church. An indirect example of this approach is found in an article published in the 1989 issue of a prominent evangelical journal. The early medieval period of the church is said to have become "entrenched in sacramentalism and moralism that did not promote a truly evangelical gospel message."[2] This was partially due to the growing emphasis on Latin as the language of the church in the early Christian era, replacing the Greek of the New Testament. The reason for the ascendancy of Latin, supposedly, was the growing domination of

1. Augustine, *Reply to Faustus the Manichaean* XXIII.5.
2. Wayne Strickland, "Seminary Education: A Philosophical Paradigm in Process," *Journal of the Evangelical Theological Society* 32 (1989): 229–30.

the Roman church, which was responsible for ushering in "un-biblical ideas" (such as sacramentalism). Because of the emphasis on Latin, the Scriptures and the Latin fathers were studied, while facility in Greek and Hebrew was lost. Just as bad, the article claims, was monasticism's stress on Latin, which helped foster "misconceptions regarding the true basis of salvation, especially since the [early] fathers were stressed over [i.e., emphasized] the Scriptures."[3]

This analysis contains disturbing features. The reader is confronted with dual presuppositions of sundering the history of Scripture from church history and the neat polarization of the church's history in terms of Reformation and pre-Reformation, the latter having its meaning only in the light of the former. Either way, we have here an all-too-familiar pattern of Scripture versus tradition (and church), the message of the first being corrupted by the second after the death of the apostles. At the heart of this paradigm is a restorationist view of church history that depicts Protestantism as the means of returning to the pure and original church of the apostles and thus legitimizing itself against the Roman Catholic claim to apostolic authority.

Since the seventeenth century, Protestant and Roman theologians have contested with each other over which "church" is the legitimate heir of the apostles and the legacy of the early fathers. Both sides have struggled to show that their faith stands in succession with what the early church held. Owen Chadwick tells the story of Sir Henry Wotton, an Anglican, visiting the church of a priest in Rome with whom he was friendly. The priest, seeing Sir Henry standing among the congregants, sent a choirboy to him with a small piece of paper on which he had written, "Where was your religion to be found before Luther?" In response, Henry wrote underneath, "My religion was to be found then, where yours is not to be found now, in the written Word of God."[4] This exchange is characteristic of what has been happening for centuries, though in more heated terms. One side focuses on the virtue of its perpetuity through church history, while the other stresses its conformity to antiquity in relation to the earliest stages of church

3. Ibid.
4. Owen Chadwick, *From Bossuet to Newman: The Idea of Doctrinal Development* (Cambridge: Cambridge University Press, 1957), 2.

history. Roman Catholics have attempted to argue for a more or less "steady-state" theory of doctrine, based on the unchanging character of its tradition and church, while Protestants have had to show, despite their criticisms of tradition and church, that they more truly represent the teaching of the ancient church. As it is, both sides have been compelled to accept the historical challenge of the other, especially since the conclusion of Vatican II. Both sides have also found that part of the challenge of history is to find points of connection with the mind of the early fathers in which Bible, tradition, and church took concrete shape.

Given that the tradition and the Bible did indeed take their first theological steps toward structure and design in the early centuries of the church, let us reconsider how these functioned as distinguishable parts and as a united authority within the church. Herein we can find some bridges over which Catholics and evangelicals may cross to the middle in conversation with each other and in respect of the future task of self-definition.

Scriptural Authority

With rare exception do the early fathers appeal to tradition independent of scriptural teaching.[5] But even in such instances, these writers are not propounding a two-source theory of revelation. In the first place, the idea that extrabiblical traditions possess the same authority as Scripture is a development of the later Middle Ages.[6] In the second place, tradition was not conceived as an addition to Scripture nor as a source that functioned apart from Scripture. No matter how much one relied on the role of the tradition to govern faith, it did not preclude the primacy of scriptural authority. The fifth-century Syrian bishop Philoxenus of Mabbug makes this clear when he says, "The truth, the accurate account, which is the lasting and steadfast, is revealed

5. Tertullian, *The Chaplet* 3; and Basil of Caesarea, *On the Holy Spirit* 66–67. Most, however, exhibited sensitivity toward the differences that existed between the tradition that had been generally received by the church from antiquity and those traditional aspects that were more peripheral to its central teaching.

6. Heiko Oberman, "Quo Vadis Petre? Tradition from Irenaeus to Humani Generis," in *The Dawn of the Reformation: Essays in Late Medieval and Early Reformation Thought*, ed. H. Oberman, 269–96 (Grand Rapids: Eerdmans, 1992).

only by the revelation of God. If one should seek something outside of these things which are set down in Scripture, one cannot understand."[7]

Under the aegis of the Holy Spirit, the Bible was the primary agent of God's ongoing work of transformation in and through the church. There was no question in the patristic mind that Scripture, in whatever version lay at hand, was the sourcebook for the wording of creeds as well as the substance for explaining the faith. Cyril of Jerusalem taught new believers that the creed (of Jerusalem) was de facto a summarization of Scripture. Indeed, one was to learn the creed because it represented an epitome of the whole Bible.

> Learn the faith and profess it; receive it and keep it—but only the Creed which the church will now deliver to you, that Creed is firmly based on Scripture. . . . For the articles of the Creed were not put together according to human choice; the most important doctrines were collected from the whole of Scripture to make up a single exposition of the faith.[8]

Each article of the creed, as Cyril expounded it, was so thoroughly grounded in biblical authority that a recent commentator on the *Catechetical Lectures* refers to Cyril as one who "subscribed to a form of *sola scriptura* doctrine."[9] Even as the bishop expounded the meaning of the creed, he insisted that his hearers not accept anything without reference to the sacred Scriptures. "Do not simply take my word when I tell you these things, unless you are given proof for my teaching from Holy Scripture."[10] Of course, it was not Cyril's intention to defend a position of *sola scriptura*, though he did want to assure his listeners that nothing in the Jerusalem creed was contrary to the biblical message. Being schooled in the creed was the first step not only in learning what the Bible meant but also in preparing candidates to read the Bible with insight.

There was no question about the supreme authority of the Holy Scripture among the early fathers. For Origen, Scripture in all its texts was the "music" of God.

7. Philoxenus, *Fragment* 28.
8. Cyril, *Catechetical Lectures* 5.12.
9. Edward Yarnold, *Cyril of Jerusalem* (London: Routledge, 2000), 56.
10. Cyril, *Catechetical Lectures* 4.17.

When a person acquainted with the music of God appears, one
who is wise both in words and deeds (Lk 7:22) . . . then this person
will produce the sound of the music of God, since he has learned
from all this how to strike the chords at the appropriate time: now
the chords of the Law, now the chords of the Gospels in harmony
with them, and now the chords of the Prophets. And when what
is reasonable demands it, he strikes also the Apostolic chords with
them, and so also the Apostolic chords with the Gospels. For this
person recognizes that all of Scripture is the one perfect and harmonious instrument of God which raises a single saving voice
from the various different sounds for the benefit of everyone who
desires to learn.[11]

But authority of Scripture was not connected with a particular
theory about the nature of the Bible. The truth and power of
the Bible were not based on a view of its inerrancy or infallibility. Scripture possessed divine character because through Scripture the sovereign will of God was at work in the world through
faith.

A critical difference between the patristic and post-Reformation
perspectives is that the former was concerned to create a view
of revelation that preserved the divine character of God, while
the latter's way of defending the Bible as the sufficiency of divine
revelation was to grant supreme authority to the text. To secure
the Bible against the claim to authority by the Roman magisterium, sixteenth- and seventeenth-century Protestantism (known
as Protestant scholasticism) constructed biblical infallibility as the
primary means of refutation.[12] Bibliology became the cornerstone
of theology. Ultimate authority lay in the Bible, so the glory of
God ought to shine through every word and syllable. Whereas for
the earlier Reformers, *sola scriptura* was a consequence of *solus
Christus* and *sola fide,* for the scholastics, *sola scriptura* was the
first principle from which Christ and faith were derived. "Luther

11. Fragment II from the *Commentary on Matthew* as preserved in the *Philocalia.*
The same author will appeal to the "canon of truth" as a necessary rule for determining
orthodox faith and trustworthy biblical interpretation.

12. For a survey of this development within Protestantism, see D. H. Williams, "Scripture, Tradition, and the Church: Reformation and Post-Reformation," in *The Free Church
and the Early Church: Essays in Bridging the Historical and Theological Divide,* ed. D. H.
Williams, 101–26 (Grand Rapids: Eerdmans, 2002).

believed in the Bible on account of Christ; Protestant scholasticism believed in Christ on account of the Bible."[13]

As a generalization about the patristic mind, it is fair to say that the fathers affirmed an infallible Bible, although it was not an infallibility of the text as much as it was an infallibility of the divine intention behind the text. Frederick Norris has observed that the fathers gave every evidence of critical intellects engaged with Scripture, as in the instance of Gospel accounts varying from one another.

> Even the tiniest difference should be explained if at all possible, but this does not depend upon a wooden understanding of inerrancy. The Fathers' sense of the trustworthy character of Scripture can have them speak about its lack of errors, but they never protect the Bible with the doctrine of inerrancy that was developed in seventeenth-century Protestantism.[14]

The early fathers did not deny the existence of historical inconsistencies, legal and moral contradictions found in the Old Testament, or conflicting accounts of the biblical writers about an event. Noah's drunken nakedness (Gen. 9), the Lord sending an evil spirit upon Saul (1 Sam. 18:10), and divinely sanctioned genocide (Num. 33:51–52) are not themselves edifying or instructive and raise the question as to why such events were included in the divine record at all. Then there are matters of conflicting accounts among scriptural authors, such as Luke telling us that the transfiguration was eight days after Jesus' prediction of his death and Mark and Matthew saying it was six. But, says Origen, just as providence is not voided because some do not accept it,

13. Carl Braaten, "A Shared Dilemma: Catholics and Lutherans on the Authority and Interpretation of Scripture," *Pro Ecclesia* 10 (2001): 66–67.

14. Frederick Norris, "The Transfiguration of Christ. The Transfiguration of the Church," in *Reading in Christian Communities: Essays on Interpretation in the Early Church*, ed. C. A. Bobertz and D. Brakke (Notre Dame: University of Notre Dame Press, 2002), 191. Norris observes that early theologians were never so deeply absorbed with intra-Christian debate that they forgot their pagan audience. Defending a totally consistent scriptural text, the same in every account, would be derided by their pagan opponents as proof of dreadful complicity. For them, both unity in faith and diversity in detail were important. John Chrysostom says, "Wasn't one gospel writer enough to tell the whole [story]? Yes, but if four write, neither at the same times, nor in the same places, neither having met each other, nor having talked about it, and then they speak as if they were one mouth, [their agreement] serves as a great proof of the truth" (ibid., 191).

so "neither is the divine character of scripture, which extends through all of it, abolished because our weakness cannot discern in every sentence the hidden splendor of its teachings."[15] In fact, such discrepancies were regarded as an opportunity for the Spirit to reveal God's power in the humble exterior of the biblical words. Divine verses could and did include literal errors since they were meant to lead to spiritual and eternal truths. We will return to the role of biblical allegory below. It is sufficient here to note that the divine character of Scripture was not dictated by trying to demonstrate the inerrancy of the text. Scriptural authority was based on the sovereign nature of God to work through the text—errors and all.

Reading Scripture by the Tradition

No matter what theory of inspiration was held, the practices of reading and hearing Scripture in the ancient church did not occur without the tradition. Again we recall the anonymous writer at the end of the first century who addressed the church at Corinth to encourage believers to avoid worldly practices and seek heartfelt repentance. Central to this exhortation, the church leaders were told to embrace "the glorious and holy canon of our tradition."[16] Here and elsewhere the writer displays no cognizance of an operational scriptural canon apart from the Old Testament, which he frequently cites as declaring fully and unambiguously the gospel of Jesus Christ. Implicit to the writer's argument is that the apostolic understanding is achieved only when Scripture is read through the lens of the "canon of our tradition," and only then does a theological and spiritual interpretation become possible. The canon or rule "of our tradition" in this instance follows the pattern of life established by Christ, very much in the same vein as Paul lays out in Galatians.

Tradition was not from outside the faith; it was regarded as the essential teaching or purport of the Bible. Therefore, Tertullian maintained that the tradition had been kept "as a sacred deposit in the churches of the apostles. . . . Let us see what milk the Cor-

15. Origen, *On First Principles* IV.1.7.
16. *1 Clement* 7.2–4.

inthians drank from Paul; to what rule (of faith) the Galatians were brought for correction; what the Philippians, the Thessalonians, the Ephesians read by it; what utterance the Romans give."[17] Tertullian, along with other second- and third-century writers, was convinced that the authors of Scripture shared an agreement about the particulars of the church's tradition or rule of faith for the simple reason that they believed the rule was the *ratio* or "scope" of scriptural revelation. This is precisely how Irenaeus understood the relationship between Scripture and the church's "rule of truth," both of which manifested the source (revelation) from which "we draw up our faith, the foundation of the building, and the consolidation of a way of life."[18]

Doctrinal historians have referred to this symbiotic relationship between Scripture and tradition as "co-inherence" (or "coincidence"),[19] since the content of the church's confessional tradition co-inhered with the content of Scripture. In the patristic mind, tradition and Scripture were comprehended in reciprocal terms. While Scripture had primacy of place for the fathers, they did not believe that Scripture could or should function in the lives of believers apart from the church's teaching and language of worship (i.e., tradition). Scripture was the authoritative anchor of tradition's content, and tradition stood as the primary interpreter of Scripture. In other words, the tradition was not a novel set of beliefs and practices added to Scripture, as if it were a separate and second revelatory source. In this vein, Thomas Aquinas asserted that the value of the biblical writers should not be separated from the early fathers, since the latter are the reliable interpreters of Scripture and the organs that continue the tradition.[20] In effect, this approach interprets the Bible by investigating and following the ancient consensus of the fathers. Their resulting theology was a theology that accurately represented the message of Scripture.

17. Tertullian, *Against Marcion* IV.5.
18. Irenaeus, *The Apostolic Preaching* 6.
19. A. N. S. Lane, "Scripture, Tradition, and Church: An Historical Survey," *Vox Evangelica* 9 (1975): 37–55; and Richard Bauckham, "Tradition in Relation to Scripture and Reason," in *Scripture, Tradition, and Reason: A Study in the Criteria of Christian Doctrine*, ed. R. Bauckham and B. Dewey, 117–45 (Edinburgh: T & T Clark, 1988).
20. John Henry Newman, ed. and trans., *Catena Aurea: Commentary on the Four Gospels* (Oxford: J. H. Parker, 1841), reprinted with an introduction by A. Nichols (London: Saint Austin Press, 1999), vii.

The tradition or apostolic preaching formed the basis of the
New Testament and served as the hermeneutical model for interpreting the Old Testament. As the body of this tradition developed
over the next three to four centuries, it was understood as that
which bears witness to and interprets Scripture. As one of my
colleagues rightly said, to follow the tradition is to affirm the
authority of Scripture. Whether it was the baptismal formulas,
catechetical summaries, or later creeds, they were valued as accurately representing the purport of Scripture. When instructing
new converts, Augustine taught, "For whatever you hear in the
Creed is contained in the inspired books of Holy Scripture." Its
content was to be written on their hearts once regenerated by
grace so that "you may love what you believe and that, through
love, faith may work in you and that you may be pleasing to the
Lord God, the Giver of all good gifts."[21]

Even works of general historical purpose contained this sensi-
bility of the coinherence of Scripture and tradition. The purpose
of Jerome's *On Illustrious Men,* as he states, was to arrange a
chronology of individuals since the time of the Lord's passion who
made a significant contribution "on [our knowledge of] the Holy
Scriptures."[22] In other words, Jerome cataloged to the best of his
knowledge the sources of all who published works of theology or
exegesis that were faithful to the tradition. To describe the tradition was inevitably to speak about the message of Scripture.

Tradition also functioned as the chief hermeneutical principle
for interpreting Scripture. Because tradition was not perceived as
possessing a content separate from scriptural teaching, the former
could act as an interpretive guide for proper use of the Bible.[23] Among
his best-known works, Augustine wrote *On Christian Teaching* (*De
doctrina Christiana*) as a guide for rightly handling and presenting
the Bible. As Augustine states in the preface, there was a need for
a clear-cut method of using the Bible because plenty of believers
in his day insisted that all they needed for arriving at an orthodox
understanding of Scripture was the personal working of the Holy

21. Augustine, *Sermon* 212.2.
22. Jerome, *On Illustrious Men* preface.
23. More than one modern scholar has commented on the obvious circularity of such
a process, and yet this dynamic was not a static one that brought the interpretive process
back to the same place. There was continual development between the two that was always
creating revisions of the tradition's content and understanding of Scripture.

Spirit. This may sound to some readers as a contemporary issue. Times may have changed, but the basic issues of arriving at an adequate knowledge of God are similar from age to age. Augustine acknowledged that some Christians would fault him for establishing certain rules (*praecepta*) for interpreting the Bible because such rules are unnecessary: "They see, or at least believe they see, that they have gained the ability to expound the holy books without recourse to any rules." Whatever illumination in understanding texts they possess, they claim it comes solely from "a special gift of God."[24]

Augustine agreed that being led by the Spirit is pivotal for biblical and theological understanding. However, it is not something that works in spiritual isolation from the shared skills of interpretation and the direction of the church's faith. For "what do we possess that we have not received from another? And if we have received it from another, why give ourselves airs, as if we had not received it?"[25] Readers were encouraged to acquire numerous tools for exposition such as a knowledge of proper grammar, reliable versions of Scripture, the meaning of the names of God, history, figures of speech, and even certain sciences—animals, plants, numbers, and so on. But most central to the interpretive task was the way in which the church's faith functioned as a hermeneutical guideline for reading the Bible. Its aim was to reveal the centrality of a "double-love," love of God and love of one's neighbor, behind the scope of scriptural teaching. By "God" was meant the "supreme good which is Trinity," and one's "neighbor" was anyone made in the image of that Trinity. Loving God as Trinity and loving one's neighbor for God's sake were to be done "from a pure heart" and "a sincere faith" (1 Tim. 1:5)[26] because an authentic love flows from a right faith. Nothing less than the "rule of faith" was necessary for directing an informed love of God as Father, Son, and Holy Spirit in order that the truth of Scripture was successfully sought. In sum, the right interpretation of the Bible is indissolubly linked to the historic faith professed in the church and to the ordering of believers' loves.[27] Without the right

24. Augustine, *On Christian Teaching* preface, 4.
25. Ibid., 17.
26. Ibid., I.95. Any Bible passage that does not overtly or implicitly support such an understanding, Augustine says, may be regarded as figurative or allegorical (ibid., III.33).
27. Ibid., III.3.

faith, wrong interpretation of the Bible, especially in regard to ambiguous or difficult passages, could only result, and one's love, however sincere, would become misguided.

Sola Scriptura?

The fathers would not have appreciated the principle of Scripture alone, since the historical and theological issues that gave rise to it were particular to late medieval Christianity.[28] To treat the Bible in isolation from the tradition of the church, as it was located in the ancient rule of faith, baptismal confessions, and conciliar creeds, would have been incomprehensible to the Christian pastors and thinkers of the patristic era. From their perspective, a radically biblicist view might easily be driven by a desire to avoid the truth of the church's teaching.[29]

One of the (unintended) hazards of "Scripture alone" is that it typifies Scripture as an isolated authority, completely independent of the church from which it emerged. Thus, *sola scriptura* has been construed by many Protestants as if finding the truth of Scripture is an enterprise best done without the church or even in spite of the church. Indeed, some parts of Protestantism have a long history of using Scripture with just such an understanding, seemingly cut off from church history.

This was, of course, not at all what the early Reformers sought to do with this theological principle. Just as Scripture is the reflection of the Word of God through Christ, so "the church has

---

28. The beginning of the end of a coinherent understanding of Scripture and tradition (and the church) is seen by the fourteenth century. George Tavard points to Henry Ghent's *Commentary on the Sentences,* written in the thirteenth century, which raised the question whether Christians are mandated to believe Scripture ("authorities of doctrine") rather than authorities of the church. Ghent supposes that if the church taught anything contrary to Scripture, believers should not believe in her but in the words of Christ. George Tavard, *Holy Writ or Holy Church* (London: Burns & Oates, 1959), 24–25. From this point, it was but a small step for the sixteenth-century Reformers.

29. This is what Augustine discovered in a public debate (in 427) with an "Arian" theologian named Maximinus. Maximinus was most insistent that his doctrine was derived solely from the Bible (Augustine, *Debate with Maximinus* 15.20). By stringing together "testimonies" (i.e., scriptural texts), Maximinus defended a subordinationist view that the Son could not be "true God" because the language in the Gospels was used only of the Father and because the Gospels spoke of the Son's nature in starkly human terms as the Word who became flesh.

everything which belongs to Christ . . . so that whatever belongs to the church belongs to Christ and whatever belongs to Christ belongs to the church."[30] Magisterial Reformers such as Luther and Calvin did not think of *sola scriptura* as something that could be properly understood apart from the church or the foundational tradition of the church, even while they were opposing some of the institutions of the church. The principle of *sola scriptura* was not intended to be *nuda scriptura*!

How should it then be understood? The early Reformers declared the Word of God, as it is communicated in Scripture, to be the final judge of all teaching of the church. But functioning as the norm of faith and practice did not mean that Scripture was the sole resource of the Christian faith. As its own history attests, Scripture is never really "alone." The church's tradition, reason, and experience are all legitimate resources that played teaching roles in the interpretation of Scripture.[31] While these resources may not share the same authority as Scripture, the notion of Scripture alone was never meant to construct the Bible as an island, as if it were a solitary resource for faith and practice. Rather, the Bible as the primary revelation of God has a place within the broader context of the Spirit's work in the world, all bearing witness to their one source.

A balanced perspective can be found in the approach of John Wesley. As a true descendent of the Reformation, Wesley argued for the importance of asserting the *sola* in *sola fide* and *sola scriptura*. He noted, however, that *solus* should be interpreted as "primarily" rather than "solely" or "exclusively." The guiding principles of Scripture and faith were never meant to be seen in isolation from the consensual and foundational tradition of the church. Wesley

30. Martin Luther, *Exposition of Psalm 45*, in *Luther's Works*, ed. T. G. Tapert and H. T. Lehmann (St. Louis: Concordia, 1955), 12.260. Unfortunately, Luther's penchant for hyperbole raises questions about his thought on the subject. For example, in *On the Babylonian Captivity*—a polemical work against papal authority—Luther said that the Word of God was incomparably superior to the church, and in this Word, "the church, being a creature, has nothing to decree, ordain, or make but only to be decreed, ordained, and made" (Martin Luther, "The Pagan Servitude of the Church" or "The Babylonian Captivity of the Church," in *Martin Luther. Selections from His Writings*, ed. J. Dillenberger [Garden City, N.Y.: Doubleday, 1961], 341).

31. A. N. S. Lane, "*Sola scriptura*? Making Sense of a Post-Reformation Slogan," in *A Pathway into the Holy Scripture*, ed. P. E. Satterthwaite and D. F. Wright, 299–313 (Grand Rapids: Eerdmans, 1994).

writes of his own early spiritual pilgrimage, "But it was not long before Providence brought me to those who showed me a sure rule of interpreting Scripture, viz., 'Consensus veterum: quod ab omnibus, quod ubique, quod semper creditum.'"[32] There was no question in his mind that the only responsible way of interpreting Scripture was through the faith of the early fathers and the historic expressions of the church. To use Scripture without this tradition was to make biblical understanding captive to every whim of personal interests and experience. He had learned from reading the fathers how often the concept of Scripture alone had been used as a platform for supporting heresy.[33]

The Scripture-only principle is no guarantee for establishing Christian truth, nor is it immune to pious and well-intentioned believers whose use and presentation of the Bible hold little connection to historic Christianity, for the Scripture-only principle could and did backfire on its adherents in the form of heretical doctrine. The Congregationalist minister Thomas Worcester published a work of theology in 1813 based solely on the Bible as the sole and supreme authority.[34] Many of his arguments in defense of biblical authority can easily be found among evangelical writers today. Worcester declared that the church had abandoned the simplicity of the gospel since the time of the apostles and had lain in darkness, error, and degeneracy. Even Luther and Calvin, who were instruments of a "great reformation," had retained too many of the formulas and words of the church's fourteen-hundred-year corruption. The major creeds of the early church should be purged from Christian faith as illicit additions to divine testimony. Relying on scriptural words alone necessitated purging most of the church's history. In doing so, Worcester found warrant to defend the doctrinal legitimacy of Unitarianism.[35]

32. A rewording of Vincent of Lérins's (*Commonitorium* II.6) well-known phrase "that which has been believed everywhere, always, and by everyone." See John Wesley, "An Early Self-Analysis," in *The Works of John Wesley*, ed. A. Outler (Nashville: Abingdon, 1984), 5.

33. Against the Moravians, Wesley adamantly rejected the idea that personal union with God is a reliable guide to interpreting the Bible.

34. Thomas Worcester, *Divine Testimony Received without Any Addition or Diminution* (Hanover, N.H.: Charles Spear, 1813).

35. Antitrinitarian theology of this time was built largely on the platform of a "return" to the primitive or apostolic church, as the writings of John Locke, Isaac Newton, and

He was not the first or the last to use *sola scriptura* toward an end that none of the Reformers had imagined.[36] Small wonder that Roman Catholics have often expressed concern about the hazardousness of the principle. On account of what it perceived as abuses of Scripture by "Protestant" movements, the Council of Trent rejected *sola scriptura* for the way it had set the Bible adrift in a sea of competing voices all claiming to speak as its genuine interpreter. In opposition to anyone who interprets Scripture according to his own understanding, the Council of Trent insisted on the preeminence of the "holy mother church, whose it is to judge the true sense and interpretation of the holy scriptures."[37] Evangelicals may not subscribe to the decisions made at Trent, but it is true that once the Bible is detached from the church and its history, the Bible becomes susceptible to anyone who claims to be speaking according to the leading of the Holy Spirit.

Another related and unintended development that has grown out of *sola scriptura* is the rampant individualism common among evangelical churches today. John Henry Newman was right when he said that Protestantism is particularly vulnerable on this score. There are a great many Christians today who think of the Bible as the believer's Bible, not the church's Bible. The plethora of Bible versions—the Women's Devotional Bible, the Mom's Devotional Bible, the Men's Bible, the Couples' Devotional Bible, the Teen Study Bible, the Kids' Study Bible, the Student's Life Application Bible, and so on—lends weight to the prevailing idea that the primary purpose of Scripture is to cater to the needs of the individual and that it can be interpreted by the Christian privately just as well as within the believing community. The number of special interest groups with their own interpretive arrangement

---

Joseph Priestly bear witness. The famous philosopher John Locke had made a similar case for the same reasons. In accordance with the views of Isaac Newton and William Whiston, both of whom had been accused of Arianism, Locke was committed to the plain text of Scripture, referring to the Council of Nicaea as the representative episode of the church's "fall" into doctrinal corruption and loss of the gospel's simplicity.

36. Such a theological tradition had already established deep roots within Protestantism and sought to return to the primitive ideals of Christianity by cleansing it from the pollutions and superstitions of Roman Catholicism. Best known in the English-speaking world was Joseph Biddle, *A Confession of Faith: Touching the Holy Trinity according to Scripture* (London: n.p., 1648).

37. "Decree Concerning the Canonical Scriptures" (*Decretum de canonicis scriptures*), from the fourth session of the council (April 8, 1546).

of the Bible is just as dizzying.[38] One would think that the familiar admonition of 2 Peter 1:20 should be taken literally: "Above all, you must understand that no prophecy of Scripture came about by the prophet's own interpretation." It appears, however, that this passage is claimed in a more oblique way by evangelicals as proving the divine character of Scripture, not condemning the privatization of biblical interpretation and application.

At the heart of this hyper-individualism are two interconnected perceptions about religion. The first is an abiding rejection of ecclesial authority. While one finds (very ironically) concrete examples of papal-like pronouncements among the Southern Baptists, most evangelicals and free churches have a morbid fear of anything episcopal. Pastoral or church authority is all very well until it makes specific demands on a believer's life and personal freedoms. The mistrust of authority has a strong cultural aspect that has as much to do with the current American mentality as it does with Christian spirituality. The key is that this symbiosis should be recognized and admitted by believers. Sociologists of religion have shown repeatedly how far a fierce individualism dictates American Christians' worldview. We are most motivated by a pattern of dispositions and practices that define life's goals in terms of personal choice, by a freedom that is framed in terms of being allowed to believe and act as one wishes, and by justice that is meant to be an opportunity for individuals to pursue happiness as each person has defined it for himself or herself.[39]

The other perception is really a misperception: that the priesthood of every believer demands the rejection of almost all religious authority. In the name of soul liberty or freedom of the conscience, some Protestants have gone to the extreme of using the priesthood of the believer as the right of the individual to decide what the Bible teaches or what practices should be embraced in the church. In this scenario, both Scripture and the church have

---

38. Besides the Charles Ryrie Study Bible there is now available *The Tim LaHaye Prophecy Study Bible, The Women of Destiny Bible, The New Spirit-Filled Life Bible, The MacArthur Study Bible, The Maxwell Leadership Bible, The Men of Integrity Bible* (Promise Keepers), and *The Life Recovery Bible* (Twelve Steps).

39. Robert Bellah et al., eds., *Habits of the Heart: Individualism and Commitment in American Life* (Berkeley: University of California Press, 1985); and Nathan O. Hatch, "The Right to Think for Oneself," in *The Democratization of American Christianity,* ed. Nathan Hatch, 162–90 (New Haven: Yale University Press, 1989).

separate spheres that need not overlap. And although Scripture is the more authoritative and binding of the two, what matters is how a believer is "called" to understand Scripture, an approach that confirms some of Trent's worst fears.

Though the Word in Scripture comes from God, it is revealed through a process in which the community of faith, appropriating both the Old and the New Testament, is profoundly involved. Indeed, it is fair to say that we will rightly hear God's Word only as we hear it in the corporate and historical voice of the church. In its final formation, the Bible came out of the life of the Christian community as it heard God's Word. What this means is that the Bible is foremost the book of the church.[40] Interpretation and realization of Scripture are ecclesiological events, and therefore the church and its tradition are integral to the handling of the Bible. This is not opposed to the principle of soul liberty as long as soul liberty does not become itself a canon of faith intended to thwart church authority as an encroachment upon religious freedom. Unfortunately, the protective aspect of soul freedom is exaggerated to distortion, admits one Baptist theologian, by the conjunction of contemporary American individualism and, since the seventeenth century, the prerogative of one's own conscience. We might concede the necessity of the latter point against a repressive hierarchy or domineering state church. "It is quite another thing, however, to witness the wholesale baptism of tendencies toward autonomous individualism by the dogma of soul freedom."[41]

In the end, believers do not believe and, more importantly, keep believing in isolation. The Bible is capable of being understood only in the midst of a disciplined community of believers whose practices embody the biblical story. As part of this embodiment, we are in need of "spiritual masters," namely, the venerable voices of the historical church whose journeys empower and enlighten our own pilgrimage toward what is authentically Christian. It is according to this understanding that the bishop Cyprian of

---

40. This is essentially the thesis behind a new series of patristic commentary on Scripture titled The Church's Bible, gen. ed., Robert L. Wilken (Grand Rapids: Eerdmans). See the first volume, Richard Norris, ed., *The Song of Songs* (Grand Rapids: Eerdmans, 2003).

41. Joel B. Green, "Biblical Authority and Communities of Discourse," in *Baptists in the Balance: The Tension between Freedom and Responsibility*, ed. E. C. Goodwin (Valley Forge, Pa.: Judson, 1997), 153.

Carthage adjured fellow clergy to instruct the congregation "according to the authority of Scripture [and] the discipline of the Church."[42]

The most crucial point to make about the ancient tradition or a shared understanding of theological canonicity is that it was not a set of theoretical principles expounded in an atmosphere of intellectual detachment. Such concepts were, in practice, indissolubly hinged to the believing, worshiping, and responsive life of the churches. Tradition, by its very name and existence, implies the "activity of the church living its belief and consequently elaborating it."[43] The *lex credendi* (rule of faith) was not something received and transmitted in isolation from its exercise within the *lex orandi* (practice of worship) or vice versa. The one was formed by the other. No assembly of ecclesiastical officials or scholarly think tanks laid down a slate of beliefs from on high and then proceeded to foist it upon the churches as worthy of their acceptance.

Scripture as Divine Mystery

To appreciate the dynamic behind the early church's understanding of Scripture and tradition, we must make some brief observations regarding the ancients' approach to Scripture. At the very least, we can see two operations at work in the patristic use of Scripture: (1) the mystical character of Scripture, and (2) the way in which the divine nature of the text calls for transformation. In both cases, the tradition and Scripture work in tandem for the formation of faith and spirituality.

Westminster Abbey offers a breathtaking vision of height and depth of, if not God, at least the experience of God of those who built the structure ten centuries ago. Certainly, worshipers have continued to share in that experience in this place. The sheer amount of space between floor and ceiling, nave and altar, as well as the complication of artistry upon every wall and window, ushers us in before a truly awesome God. His goodness, mercy, and love notwithstanding, God will not be domesticated by our

---

42. Cyprian, *Epistle* 5.2.

43. Yves Congar, *Tradition and Traditions: An Historical and Theological Essay* (New York: Macmillan, 1967), 5.

warm religiousness or boxed-in by our intellectual conceptions. One thinks of the figure of Aslan in C. S. Lewis's Chronicles of Narnia, whose goodness and grandeur defy containment because, as Mr. Tumnus once said, he's not a tame lion!

For many Protestants, one of the most problematic sides to patristic use of the Bible is the fathers' predilection toward allegorical and mystical interpretation of the text. Of all of Luther's problems with the early church, he saw its allegorizing of the Bible as the biggest obstacle to sound scriptural understanding. He especially objected to the works of Origen, who justified allegory as the exegesis of the mature and faithful believer. The imaginative interpretation of Scripture permitted by allegorical method could lead to its haphazard use in defense of seemingly any teaching. Ambrose of Milan, for example, tells his congregation that in the story of the cleansing of Naaman's leprosy (2 Kings 5:1–14), the captive girl who advised him to submit himself to the prophet Elisha is "the church of the Lord, once humiliated by the captivity of sin." Thanks to her (the church's) counsel, now "the foolish people of the pagans have listened to the prophetic word (the gospel) about which they had previously entertained doubts."[44]

It was apparent, therefore, that the allegorizing of Scripture had to be harnessed by the more obvious or literal realities of the passage. Many Protestant thinkers after Luther followed suit: Allegorical or spiritual interpretation of the Bible lacks a clear method and the predictability that exegesis is supposed to supply. In whatever way the apostolic authors utilized allegorical and typological exegesis, it was not a model that could be readily emulated by those who came after them.[45] The result was an approach to the Bible and its preaching that stressed the historical and literal reading of Scripture to the point of making it ultimately normative. In Luther's eyes, the Holy Spirit is the simplest writer and advisor: "That is why his words [Scripture] could have no more than one simplest meaning which we call the written one or the literal meaning of the tongue."[46] Critical methods of exegesis

---

44. Ambrose, *On the Mysteries* 3.18.

45. As discussed in Richard Longnecker, *Biblical Exegesis in the Apostolic Period* (Grand Rapids: Eerdmans, 1975).

46. Martin Luther, *Concerning the Letter and the Spirit*, in *Martin Luther's Basic Theological Writings*, ed. T. F. Lull (Minneapolis: Fortress, 1989), 78.

that emerged from the biblical studies of the late nineteenth and twentieth centuries were built upon the normalizing of historical and literal interpretation.

Allegorical or spiritual interpretation of passages was frowned upon as an illegitimate use of the Bible since it seemed imposed rather than discovered. As the derisive saying goes, "Allegorical exegesis is like a picnic; one person brings the text and someone else brings the meanings, but the two are prepared in different kitchens."[47] Protestants worried that an allegorical use of the Bible could supply the warrant for any number of traditions that the church wanted to justify by Scripture. It was bad enough that Romanists had argued that early church traditions offered sanction for extra-scriptural teaching, but it was even worse to find scriptural support through exegetical gymnastics of meaning.[48] So Protestants came to identify the spiritual sense of Scripture with human teaching originating in the dogmas of the church rather than scriptural teaching.

For ancient Christian thinkers, every passage had more than one meaning precisely because it was inspired by the Holy Spirit. Therefore, getting to the point of a text required careful deliberation and a submissive attitude. According to patristic writers, looking for a purely literal interpretation did not do justice to the sacred nature of Scripture. Instead, they claimed that points of obscurity or even contradiction within the Bible provided an opportunity for the Spirit to work in a Christian heart because the dilemma was more than the human mind could comprehend. Such problems were not obstacles to be overcome by manipulating the text but open doors by which only the faithful could discover the power of God in ways not obvious to the unconverted or a carnal believer. Augustine, for example, explained in one of his sermons that obscure or conflicting passages in Scripture exist not because God wants to conceal his mysteries from us but "because he only wants to open them up to those who are prepared to look for them." Such texts are meant "to spur us on, heart and soul,

47. Cited in Robert L. Wilken, "Interpreting Job Allegorically: The *Moralia* of Gregory the Great," *Pro Ecclesia* 10 (2001): 215.

48. J. Z. Smith, *Drudgery Divine: On the Comparison of Early Christianity and the Religions of Late Antiquity* (London: School of Oriental and African Studies, University of London, 1990), chap. 3.

to the search."[49] This is what Jesus meant, Augustine asserted, when he said, "Do not give dogs what is sacred; do not throw your pearls to pigs" (Matt. 7:6).

A literal interpretation of the Bible was not an insurance policy against abuse of the Bible's meaning. It might serve as a means of determining a valid explanation in conjunction with other methods, but it should not stand alone. In his sermons on various scriptural passages, the fifth-century pastor Peter Chrysologus claimed, "The historical narrative should always be raised to a higher meaning (*intelligentiam*), and mysteries of the future should become known through figures of the present. Therefore, we should unfold by allegorical discourse what mystical teaching is contained beneath the outward appearance [of the text]."[50] The purpose of sound exegesis, therefore, is to "elevate its historical sense to a mystical and extraordinary sense which God gave it."[51] While the literal meaning should not be cast aside as irrelevant, it was perfected by the spiritual understanding. Gregory the Great put it this way:

> Allegory, after all, devises for the sake of the soul that is far removed from God, a stratagem that will elevate it to God. When the figurative language is interposed, the soul, even while it grasps in the words something on its own level, apprehends in their intelligible sense something that is not on its own level, and by earthly words is separated from what is earthly. . . . The divine teachings are clothed in things that are familiar to us; the things out of which allegories are made. And as we consider the exterior words, we achieve an interior discernment.[52]

A literal or historical meaning can be perceived by anyone, but only a spiritually oriented believer can discern the spiritual depths that exist in a text. To know nothing but the letter of the text (the literal meaning), Origen once argued, is to be like one of the Pharisees or scribes on whom Jesus pronounced "woe" (Matt. 23:13). This is because one will construe the gospel in the same

49. Augustine, *Sermon* 60A.
50. Peter Chrysologus, *Sermon* 36.
51. Ibid., 5.
52. Gregory the Great, *Expositio in Canticis Canticorum* 3, in *Song of Songs*, 8.

way as the law, not realizing that Jesus Christ as the Word is the fulfillment of God's promises. Instead, the reader should:

> upon receiving a passage through the letter of the Scriptures, proceed to ascend higher to the spiritual matters, which are called the Kingdom of Heaven. . . . And only according as each thought is attained and perceived in an exalted fashion, and moreover demonstrated and revealed can one perceive the Kingdom of Heaven.[53]

But just as significant was the recognition that the task of scriptural interpretation is dependent on the principles of the Christian faith as found in the rule of faith or the creed of one's baptism. When it comes to allegorical or spiritual interpretations, not any meaning ascribed to a text will do. A mystical rendering of biblical passages ought not to be at the beck and call of the interpreter such that a text will prove almost any teaching of the church. In various summary forms, this "faith" functioned as the hermeneutical center of the task of interpreting texts. The faith of the church both guided and was responsive to the text of the Bible.

Text's Mystical Character Shows the Depth and Greatness of God

The patristic hermeneutic could be haphazard, but it was not a matter of allegorizing this or that biblical passage as much as it was an entire theological vision. The various approaches to discovering meaning or "senses" thought to be inherent in Scripture were partly the basis of formulating this vision, which is what made it possible to discern relationships between God and history, Christ and the church, and theology and spirituality. These "senses" varied among three (literal, moral, and mystical or spiritual) or four (literal, moral, anagogical, and allegorical),[54] but the basic idea was the same: God "built" these possible interpretations into Scripture for the edification and growth of his

---

53. Origen, *Commentary on Matthew* X.14.

54. There was no uniform approach in the ancient or medieval period; Origen and Jerome followed a tripartite division, whereas a quadripartite delineation is exemplified by Clement of Alexandria, Augustine, and John Cassian. For a description of the exegetical senses, see Susan Wood, *Spiritual Exegesis and the Church in the Theology of Henri de Lubac* (Grand Rapids: Eerdmans, 1998), 27–46.

people. Indeed, the scriptural senses reflected the nature of God himself. Ambrose explained at the beginning of his commentary on Luke that the "threefold wisdom" (natural or literal, moral, and spiritual) found in the Bible originates from the Trinity.

> We must believe in that Father who of his nature begot for us the Redeemer; and in that moral Son who redeemed us, being obedient to the Father until death according to his manhood; and in that rational Spirit who instills in human hearts the rationale for worshipping the Deity governing our lives.[55]

The art of writing comments on the biblical text in a line-by-line or passage-by-passage format began around the time of the mid-third century with Origen of Alexandria. Of course, Eastern and Western writers had previously commented upon the Bible with analytical and applicable goals in mind. At the end of the second century, Tertullian offered concerted remarks about the Lord's Prayer in Matthew 5 as he was writing about the subject of prayer. Cyprian did the same. Scripture was also the main tool used when it came to warding off pagan attacks or refuting Christian heresy. A number of scriptural commentaries came from the pen of Hippolytus or from his circle in Rome.[56] But it was Origen who singlehandedly made writing biblical commentaries a staple of understanding how the church's faith was informed by and informed the use of Scripture. By the time of his death, Origen had produced, besides works of theology and hundreds of homilies, passage-by-passage commentaries on the Pentateuch; the Major and Minor Prophets; Psalms and Song of Songs; the Gospels of Matthew, Luke, and John; and the Pauline Epistles. His writings soon become the standard that later commentators, East and West, emulated and by which they gauged the quality of their own contributions.

For Origen, Scripture is simultaneously plain and mysterious because it was given by God's hand. This double-sided character to Scripture is testimony to its divinity, though were it not for the depths of meaning that only an allegory can bring, one would never grasp the inspirational nature of the Bible, especially the

---

55. Ambrose, *Commentary on Luke* prologue, 5.
56. For the Hippolytan corpus, see *Patrology* II.165–94.

Old Testament.[57] In other words, the divine character of Scripture is revealed through a spiritual understanding inherent to the text.[58]

Scriptural simplicity is such that anyone who lacks an education or is a new Christian can understand it for salvation. It also has a deep and profound side that carries spiritual and allegorical meaning that only a believer can fathom through the pursuit of wisdom and personal purity. This is no accident or mere philosophical arrangement in Origen's eyes. Both "sides" of the Bible are designed by God to work this way, marking the difference between the pagan or carnal Christian and the spiritually sensitive believer who is making good progress in the Christian faith. In fact, the divine authors of the Bible purposely inserted "certain stumbling blocks, as it were" (such as contradictions or ethical inconsistencies) into the text, prompting the discerning reader to search for the meaning that is hidden.[59] It follows that the hidden meaning will be concealed from many readers. Because "the Scriptures were composed by the Spirit of God, they have not only that meaning which is obvious, but also another which is hidden from the majority of readers."[60]

Many of my students are surprised by this approach to the Bible. One voiced her opinion by complaining that it did not seem democratic enough. It is unfair, she said, that not everyone who reads the Bible is equally able to comprehend it. She is not alone in this belief. For most Protestants, egalitarian and populist assumptions are at work when it comes to interpreting the Bible. Such a point is related to its translation into vernacular languages during the fifteenth and sixteenth centuries, thus releasing the biblical text from the privileged few who could read Latin or Greek. And while it is true that the Bible is "everyman's book," the basis of its deeper understanding is not at all a democratic enterprise.

57. Origen, *On First Principles* IV.1.6.

58. For richly faceted and many textured is the planting of the words contained throughout all of Scripture. And as for the treasure that was hidden in the field (Matt. 13:44), this means the thoughts that are concealed and resting beneath what is plainly visible: namely, the thoughts of the wisdom concealed in a mystery and in Christ (1 Cor. 2:7), in whom are the concealed treasures of wisdom and knowledge (Col. 2:3) (Origen, *Commentary on Matthew* X.5).

59. Origen, *On First Principles* IV.2.9.

60. Ibid., I.8.

Origen declared that any interpretation of Scripture always requires God's assistance. But this is especially true for an interpretation that goes beyond the basic or literal rendering of a passage. Following the apostle Paul's words in 1 Corinthians 2:10, Origen taught that a penetrating look into the deeper meaning of Scripture is wholly beyond the power of man, requiring the Spirit of Christ. The Spirit reveals Christ to us in all matters, so just as no one knows the things of God except the Spirit of God, no one knows the things spoken by Christ in proverbs and parables unless he shares in the mind of Christ (1 Cor. 2:11). With a sensitivity that divine wisdom comes to us through the working of the Trinity, Origen observed that all wisdom for understanding Scripture is given by God through the Spirit, who reveals Christ. What this means is that one's position of holiness before a holy God has everything to do with comprehending Holy Writ. Those more accustomed to looking upon divine things are better able to discern the divine hand in Scripture.

Divine Nature of the Text Calls for Transformation

Sharing in the mystical or allegorical reading of Scripture is to invite the Spirit of God to work in one's heart. As Origen stated in his Matthew commentary, "But whenever someone draws near so as to make room for the Word, then the kingdom of Heaven draws near to such a person."[61] The use of spiritual or allegorical interpretation was not a hermeneutical "escape hatch" designed to help people get around the meaning of problematic passages without having to face them. The point of it, in the end, was to draw believers deeper into the life of God. As the "letter kills," the "Spirit gives life" (2 Cor. 3:6), a "life" of understanding that enables pilgrims to perceive the works of God for what they are. In effect, the purpose of the mystical or spiritual understanding of the Bible is the transformation of believers.

Because the early church did not bifurcate the intellectual and the practical to the same extent we do today, transformation of believers through Scripture was a moral and rational exercise. In a collection about ascetics' lives, a work known as the *Lausiac History*, Palladius says that the soul of the one who loves God

---

61. Origen, *Commentary on Matthew* X.14.

should desire to hear his Word. The proper approach to reading Scripture was first to purge the body of all uncleanness, feelings of pride, and boastfulness (Prol. 14). Holy Scripture must be read by those who are holy, which is the only way that some understanding of God will result.[62] Without the pursuit of physical purity one can gain only the most superficial understanding of the Bible. In other words, one will be capable of grasping only the surface (i.e., literal) meaning of the text, which breeds shallowness.

Intellectual and spiritual purity were also necessary in order that the "eyes of the heart" may "see" God. This is a frequent refrain of Origen, who appealed to Matthew 5:8: "Blessed are the pure in heart, for they will see God."

> For what else is "to see God in the heart" but to understand and know Him with the mind . . . for there are in us two kinds of senses, the one being mortal, corruptible and human [i.e., the literal sense], and the other immortal, intellectual and what is called the divine [i.e., the spiritual sense]. By this divine sense, therefore, not of the eyes but of a pure heart, that is, the mind, God can be seen by those who are worthy.[63]

Origen's argument was not meant to undermine the sensible or surface realities of which the text speaks, as if he were creating a stark dualism between the sensible and the spiritual. Doing so would invite the spiritual meaning to become a free flight of interpretive fancy, confirming Luther's deepest misgivings. For Origen, however, there is a profound relationship between apparent and nonapparent scriptural meanings. This is because there exists in Scripture an inner "order" or "coherence" that links the two and presents a compatibility of these two dimensions of meaning.[64] While anyone can derive benefit from the surface narrative of the biblical text, as do the "the multitudes of sincere and simple believers," there is always the danger either that one will find the text satisfying as it stands and learn nothing truly divine (i.e., see the text as nothing more than a narrative) or that

---

62. Robert T. Meyer, "*Lectio Divina* in Palladius," in *Kyriakon: Festschrift Johannes Quasten*, vol. 1 (Münster: Verlag Aschendorff, 1970), 580–84.

63. Origen, *On First Principles* I.1, 9.

64. John David Dawson, *Christian Figural Reading and the Fashioning of Identity* (Berkeley: University of California Press, 2002), 58.

the morally questionable or illogical aspects of the narrative will drive the reader away as seemingly unworthy of God.

This is exactly what happened to Augustine when he first read the Bible as a young man. Its unattractive style of Latin, the accounts of Abraham's repeated lies about his wife, and bloody sacrifices as a means of appeasing God convinced him that catholic Christianity was a crude and base religion.[65] Not until Augustine heard the sermons of the bishop Ambrose and learned that the surface of the text was one dimension that could be opened by the spiritual did he begin to embrace the Bible as an authority and intellectually feasible.

Because of the ordered interrelationship between the sensible (surface) and the nonsensible aspects of the biblical narrative, the spiritually enlightened reader is able to find coherent connections in the text of Scripture (in words, images, stories, parables, etc.). Just as God prompted the human authors to write, so the Spirit's task is to bring the literal and sensible realities into alignment with the spiritual metanarrative. That is, the literal must be regarded in the light of the much broader narrative of God's creation, redemption, and re-creation. "The allegorical reader then reads the narrative of Scripture in order to discern this spiritual metanarrative (which is the deepest 'meaning' of the text and its inner coherence."[66] Therefore, Origen asks, "How can one be said to believe the Scripture in the proper sense, when he does not perceive the meaning of the Holy Spirit in it, which God wants to be believed rather than the intent of the letter?"[67] There is every reason, therefore, for readers to look for deeper meanings and, within the boundaries of Scripture's unity, to draw upon them. As readers make these discernments, they find themselves transformed by the true teaching of the Word.

In sum, the above inquiry is not an *apologia* for the use of allegory. Today's readers of the Bible should always have a respectful hesitation before engaging in spiritual interpretation of most biblical passages. Unfortunately, many Protestant expositors and contemporary writers of biblical commentaries have gone too far in the opposite direction. The flexibility of postmodern exegesis

65. Augustine, *Confessions* III.5, 9.
66. Dawson, *Christian Figural Reading and the Fashioning of Identity,* 59–60.
67. Origen, *Commentary on John* 10.300.

notwithstanding, evangelical writers tend to present the science of scriptural interpretation, implicitly or explicitly, in ways hostile to the allegorical. As a result, evangelicals often have little appreciation for, if not repugnance toward, the patristic use of the Bible. It is necessary, therefore, to reduce the alienation many evangelicals experience when they read the early fathers by discussing the rationale behind allegorical exegesis. More importantly, the point of this chapter has been to show how Scripture was functioning when methods of interpretation were at their formative stages and how that interpretation was shaped by Scripture's place within the church's tradition. Not all interpretations of a passage were acceptable to the ancients given the way the rest of Scripture and the tradition served as theological parameters that effectively limited the possible number of interpretations. Of course, there was latitude in the kinds of images and ideas a particular text could conjure, but there was a certain hermeneutical "fence" that kept the mystical use of the Bible relatively confined to the conceptional and terminological world of the canonical Scripture.[68]

Affirming the Mystery

The Christian faith for the last millennium and a half has acknowledged and built on the wonderful mystery that is God and his revelation to us. While the frequently stated goal of evangelical piety is to "know" Christ as Lord and Savior, evangelicals must be mindful of what such knowledge does and does not mean. Confidence in attaining divine knowledge is easily threatened by the emphasis that other Christian traditions place on the mystery of God and our inability to apprehend his greatness. The Syriac Christian poet Ephraem of Nisibis reminds us:

> Let us not allow ourselves to go astray
>   and to study our God.
> Let us take the measure of our mind,
>   and gauge our thinking.
> And as for our knowledge, let us know how small it is, and
> Too contemptible to scrutinize the Knower of all.

68. See chap. 2 for the meaning of the canonical Scripture in the patristic age.

Seal your mouth with silence; let your tongue not act rashly.
    Know yourself, a creature made, a child of one so fashioned,
That there is a great chasm
Between you and the Son, at the edge of scrutiny.[69]

Notice that the "chasm" between creature and Creator is not something to be overcome or removed as problematic to the Christian life. God's sending his Son incarnate demonstrates that the chasm is one of (our) knowledge and not one of love. The incarnate Word of God becomes himself the "bridge," as Ephraem later calls him, to the Father. This is what one encounters in the whole teaching of Scripture, which itself enables our understanding of God's revelation. But Scripture too contains the mystery in the form of words, describing the works of God that are disclosed to human minds only by grace. Throughout the divine text are divine meanings and hidden realities that exceed our knowledge. "Religious thought or 'theology' then rightfully consists in the contemplation of the 'mystery,' the mystic symbols in which God reveals the truth about himself and the world."[70]

For Protestants to read the early fathers, who will help them read their Bibles, the door to joyful mystery must be opened. Knowledge, even the knowledge that comes from Scripture, is not undermined but humbled as it is situated before the awesome depths of God.

---

69. Quoted from Sidney Griffith, *"Faith Adoring the Mystery": Reading the Bible with St. Ephraem the Syrian* (Milwaukee: Marquette University Press, 1997), 22.
    70. Ibid., 30.

PROTESTANT TRADITION
AND THE CHRISTIAN TRADITION

Bid me to live, and I will live
Thy Protestant to be.

H. M. Herrick

OR THE PROTESTANT mind, any serious dialogue about the Christian tradition must address the way in which a believer is made righteous by faith. The doctrinal hallmark of the sixteenth-century Reformation, that God's righteousness is bestowed upon sinners only by faith through the unmerited grace of Christ, has operated as the very linchpin of orthodox Christian teaching. "Nothing in this article," Luther once declared, "can be given up or compromised, even if heaven and earth should be destroyed,"[1] a conviction articulated in the Augsburg Confes-

1. Martin Luther, *Exposition of Psalm 117*, in *Luther's Works*, ed. T. G. Tapert and H. T. Lehmann (St. Louis: Concordia, 1955), 14.37. Cf. Smalcald Articles II.1 (1537): It is the "first and chief article" of the church.

115

sion (1530) with the more famous words "justification by grace through faith alone" (*sola fide*). Since then, these words have been echoed by Lutheran, Reformed, and many other Protestant communions as the primary hermeneutic for rightly comprehending the whole of the Bible.

This teaching has not simply stood still as a Protestant memorial frozen in time, however. Taking a developmental approach toward doctrine, theologians have sought to articulate the main factors for its emergence in the sixteenth century. Considerable strides have been made between Lutherans and Roman Catholics during the last decade in determining the negotiable and nonnegotiable aspects of justification by faith. Following a visit of Pope John Paul II to Munich in 1980, a joint ecumenical commission formed of Roman Catholic and Protestant (Lutheran, Reformed, and United) church leaders in Germany undertook an exploration of factors that had led to the doctrinal condemnations in the sixteenth century and inquired whether these factors still applied.[2] It was generally agreed that the doctrine of justification "remains the central task in all attempts to arrive at an understanding between the Roman Catholic church and the churches of the Reformation."[3] Meanwhile, ecumenical study sessions were held between the Vatican and the World Federation of Lutherans throughout the 1970s and 1980s, producing a number of theological position papers.[4]

An ecumenical landmark was achieved on October 31, 1999, when subscribing Lutheran churches and the Roman Catholic Church signed "The Joint Declaration on the Doctrine of Justification" in Augsburg, agreeing on a common articulation of justification by God's grace through faith in Christ. The declaration was not intended to cover all the points that either church teaches about justification. Rather, the declaration presented a "consensus on the basic truths of the doctrine of justification"

---

2. The results of this commission were published in German in 1986. See also the English version: Karl Lehmann and Wolfhart Pannenberg, eds., *The Condemnations of the Reformation Era: Do They Still Divide?* trans. Margaret Kohl (Minneapolis: Fortress, 1989).

3. Ibid., 36.

4. H. G. Anderson et al., *Justification by Faith: Lutherans and Catholics in Dialogue VII* (Minneapolis: Augsburg, 1985). In 1989 and 1990, two volumes of essays supporting this endeavor were published, though papers from this collection did not appear in English for another decade.

and showed that the remaining differences "are no longer the occasion for doctrinal condemnations." Issued under the authority of the Lutheran World Federation and the Pontifical Council for Promoting Christian Unity, the declaration proclaimed the following:

> In faith we together hold the conviction that justification is the work of the triune God. The Father sent his Son into the world to save sinners. The foundation and presupposition of justification is the incarnation, death and resurrection of Christ. Justification thus means that Christ himself is our righteousness, in which we share through the Holy Spirit in accord with the will of the Father. Together we confess: By grace alone, in faith in Christ's saving work and not because of any merit on our part, we are accepted by God and receive the Holy Spirit, who renews our hearts while equipping and calling us to good works.[5]

As a result of the common consensus, the teaching of Lutheran churches and the teaching of the Roman Catholic Church no longer stand in condemnation of each other (*JD*, 26). This is indeed a monumental step in the saga of twentieth-century ecumenism and should be welcomed by all Protestants who value catholicity. On this most pivotal point of Christian doctrine, these longtime adversaries no longer have to regard each other's position as the diametrical "other." As Avery Dulles has observed, the declaration dispels some false stereotypes: Lutherans cannot charge Roman Catholics with holding that justification is a human achievement rather than a divine gift, and Roman Catholics cannot accuse Lutherans of believing that justification by faith does not involve inner renewal or good works.[6]

At the same time, the declaration is not an initiative that leads to full communion between both churches, nor does it annul the existence of differences over other doctrines related to justification by faith (the Word of God, the church, ministry, and the sacraments). The two church partners, rather, are committed to continued and deepened study of the biblical foundations of

---

5. *Gemainsame Erklärung zur Rechtfertigungslehre* (Frankfurt am Main: Otto Lembeck, 1999); and *The Joint Declaration on the Doctrine of Justification* (Grand Rapids: Eerdmans, 2000), 15, hereafter *JD*.

6. Avery Dulles, "Two Languages of Salvation," *First Things* 98 (1999): 26.

justification, sharing a unity in diversity and a common witness in the interpretation of the message of justification for all people (*JD*, 42). Other dialogues of a similar nature are also continuing.[7] In the United States, informal agreements have been reached between evangelicals and Roman Catholics. Most notable is the statement on salvation by Evangelicals and Catholics Together titled "The Gift of Salvation."[8] Of the seven paragraphs that specifically address justification, the following affirmations are especially noteworthy for the way in which Protestant language has been preserved in an ecumenical statement.

> We agree that justification is not earned by any good works or merits of our own; it is entirely God's gift. . . . In justification, God, on the basis of Christ's righteousness alone, declares us to be no longer his rebellious enemies but his forgiven friends, and by virtue of his declaration it is so.
> We understand that what we here affirm is in agreement with what the Reformation traditions have meant by justification by faith alone (*sola fide*).

Still, not enough has been said for those who harbor a deep concern that the current dialogues with Roman Catholicism threaten to undermine the historic distinctives of the Reformation's assertion of justifying faith.[9] A renewed defense of the Lutheran position has been given by Eberhard Jüngel, who claims that the "Joint Declaration" reconstructs only a superficial agreement between the Reformation churches and the Roman Catholic Church. Whatever doctrinal rapprochement has been fashioned between the

7. A consultation that convened from November 26–December 1, 2003, between the Lutheran World Federation, the World Alliance of Reformed Churches, the World Methodist Council, and Roman Catholics is ongoing.

8. *Christianity Today* (December 8, 1997): 34. The same working group published "Christian Mission in the Third Millennium," *First Things* 43 (1994): 15–22.

9. A sense of betrayal of the Reformation principles by the evangelicals who signed the latter is illustrated in R. C. Sproul, *Faith Alone: The Evangelical Doctrine of Justification* (Grand Rapids: Baker, 1995), for whom "the Reformation" is defined by the theology of Luther and Calvin, more or less equating their theology with "the biblical gospel" (e.g., 43–44). It is quite striking that Sproul nowhere addresses the meticulous dialogues on justification by faith between the Lutherans and Roman Catholics that have been published since 1983. A more balanced and historically informed defense of the same issues can be found in Carl Braaten, *Justification: The Article by Which the Church Stands or Falls* (Minneapolis: Fortress, 1990).

two churches, the theological deficiencies of the Roman Church as defined by the Council of Trent cannot be sidestepped. The sixteenth-century definition of justification by faith alone is absolutely central to maintaining the integrity of the Christian message of grace.[10] Some Protestant apologists from the ranks of evangelicals more forcefully proclaim justification by faith in the terms of the Augsburg Confession as the only legitimate form of expressing the gospel. Justification by faith is the doctrinal axis around which all other Christian doctrines turn.

In reaction to the Evangelicals and Catholics Together statement, a paper was recently produced by evangelical scholars and activists called "The Gospel of Jesus Christ: An Evangelical Celebration." It declared that the "doctrine of imputation (reckoning or counting) both our sins to Christ and of his righteousness to us . . . is essential to the biblical Gospel" (art. 12). It is not sufficient that one accept the theological necessity that a sinner is justified by faith. A specific theory of how justification works—a forensic declaration of God's righteousness and that justification and sanctification are two entirely distinguishable acts in salvation—must be adopted as the only faithful biblical understanding. Inherent to this understanding is the reaffirmation of Luther's establishment of Pauline theology as a *sine qua non* of the Christian message. In effect, justification by faith as articulated in Paul's letters (or at least how Luther and his successors interpreted it) is *the* teaching of the New Testament and of the gospel.[11] These are strong statements that place particular Reformation perspectives about justification on par with biblical teaching. It is one thing to insist

10. Eberhard Jüngel, *Justification: The Heart of the Christian Faith*, trans. J. F. Cayzer (Edinburgh: T & T Clark, 2001). In particular, he says that the Roman and Lutheran positions about the ability of the fallen human free will (*imago Dei*) to choose the good as it is related to justification are incompatible. Any "active participation" on the part of sinners for their justification by means of a prevenient grace must be excluded by a view true to the intent of the Reformation.

11. Luther was consistent with his doctrinal position in declaring that the New Testament documents are not all equal in their authority. In the preface to his German translation of the New Testament, he ranks the importance of New Testament books, arguing that the "true essence of the gospel" is found in John's Gospel and first epistle, Paul's epistles (especially Romans, Galatians, and Ephesians), and 1 Peter. These are said to be superior and much preferred over the three other Gospels and other books of the New Testament. Thus, the "tradition" of justification by faith as stated by Luther was the determination of a biblical canon within a canon, an outcome that many evangelicals today have ignored in their stress on the centrality of the justification by faith doctrine.

that justification by faith is a major aspect of the gospel, but it is quite another to equate it with the gospel. Jüngel goes so far as to state that Paul's opposition to Peter's legalism in Galatians 2 is "after a fashion, the birth of Protestant theology."[12]

How should we regard the teaching of justification by faith in light of the great tradition? Does it see justification by faith alone as the single most important criterion for interpreting the Christian faith? This chapter invites readers to consider some interpretative issues as they pertain to the role of justifying faith in the early tradition and their implications for an evangelical understanding of doctrinal authority. Just as we discussed the way in which the Protestant principle of Scripture alone (*sola scriptura*) has been related to the historic tradition, here we consider the same as it concerns justification by faith (*sola fide*). For most Protestants, *sola fide* is inextricably connected to *sola scriptura* in that the former is the theological outcome of the latter. Assuming this is true, it is no less important to look at the teaching of justification in light of its roots in the early church and to see how grace, as an undeserved gift of God, granted through the Son and imparted by the Spirit into the lives of believers, fits into the larger scheme of Christian faith. Thus, the next few pages show that justification has precedents in the patristic church and that, more significantly, the early fathers have much to tell us about understanding the doctrine of justifying faith within the whole counsel of biblical and Christian teaching.

The Reformers and the Past

There is no question that the early Reformers believed they were seeking to restore the faith of the early church. The basic thrust of their mission was to point not to themselves as the begetters of a new "protestantism" but to the establishment of a proper catholicism—anti-Roman perhaps but not anti-catholic. The guiding theological precedent was the fifteenth-century martyr Jan Hus, who had declared that the work of the Spirit was realized in the activity of the early church, apostolic and patristic. "We do not intend to explain Scripture otherwise than the Holy Spirit

12. Jüngel, *Justification*, 2.

and than it is explained by the holy doctors to whom the
·it gave understanding."

> 1 his law [of redemption] did not fail for governing the
> ing devoted priests ministered this law unto the people,
> w   d the judgment of holy doctors, which judgment they
> iss   :ndwelling of the Holy Spirit as is clear from the cases
> of \ ._ Augustine, St. Jerome, St. Gregory and St. Ambrose, who
> were given after the apostles' death to the church to teach her.[13]

In matters of historical continuity, the fathers were truly the successors of Peter and Paul. In fact, Hus declared, whatever doctrinal matters the early fathers agreed upon, the Roman hierarchy may not lawfully declare the opposite.

While it is not exactly clear how much Luther was indebted to Hus's ideas, Luther did perceive himself walking in Hus's footsteps, averring in 1520 that "we are all Hussites—even Paul and Augustine are literally Hussites."[14] Hus represented for him a genuine image of the early faith that had to be reclaimed. Although Luther did not emphasize the Spirit's working through the fathers, as did his hero, he did make a distinction between the normative tradition laid down in the early church and the practices espoused by the Roman Catholic Church in the name of tradition.

Exemplifying this distinction, Luther wrote in a letter to the Christians at Halle:

> I shall not cite here the sayings of the other saintly fathers, such
> as Cyprian . . . or Irenaeus, Tertullian, Chrysostom, etc. Rather I
> wish to confine myself solely to the canon law of popes and the
> Roman church, upon whose ordinances, usages, and tradition they
> so mightily depend and insist. They have to admit that they stand
> in contradiction to God's word, Christ's ordinances, Paul's teachings, and the usages of earlier popes and the usages of the early
> Roman church, and all the holy fathers and teachers.[15]

13. Jan Hus, *The Church by John Hus,* trans. David Schaff (New York: Charles Scribner's Sons, 1915), 149.

14. Scott Hendrix, "We Are All Hussites? Hus and Luther Revisited," *Archiv für Reformationsgeschichte* 65 (1974): 134.

15. Martin Luther, "A Letter of Consolation to the Christians at Halle," in *Luther's Works,* 43.156.

Scholars have justly proposed that the Reformation was essentially about reclaiming sacred history, as the church had repeatedly fallen away from its original foundations and stood in need of correction.[16] For some reforming movements, such as many Anabaptist groups, the utter corruption of the church required a radical revision of history that nullified the relevance of most of it. But given the Roman charge of innovation against the Reformers—that they were inventing a new church (no more defamatory charge could be cast at one's opponents in the medieval ages)—the latter could not afford to jettison church history and maintain a credible ecclesiology.

In Luther's mind, the church's past was the vital "stuff" of Reformation. Addressing the corruption of the present church meant that a tangible means of showing continuity with the early church was necessary, though it could not be done without discernment. On the matter of justification by faith, he was not afraid to criticize the fathers when he thought some of them had not attained a proper understanding of it. Luther once declared that it is hard to find in the writings of Origen and Jerome even three lines that teach the doctrine of justification. The same problem would have befallen Augustine "if the Pelagians had not eventually exercised his full attention and driven him to the righteousness that is of faith."[17] Yet Luther admitted in the beginning of his lecture on Genesis (1535) that he learned of justification by faith through Scripture and also found it in Augustine, Hilary, Cyril, and Ambrose. Augustine, most of all, was to be regarded as the most faithful expositor of St. Paul. Throughout his life, Luther maintained the view that Augustine's late theology was an irreducibly valid theology to which the church needed to conform.[18] It was Augustine's anti-Pelagian works that Luther read so closely and with which he identified his own struggles. Whenever forces in the church trust in the power of human beings to save themselves and do not cast themselves utterly upon God's merciful grace, the

16. Bruce Gordon, "The Changing Face of Protestant History in the Sixteenth Century," in *Protestant History and Identity in Sixteenth-Century Europe*, vol. 1, ed. B. Gordon (Aldershot: Scolar Press, 1996), 3–4.

17. Martin Luther, *Exposition on the Prophet Amos*, in *Luther's Works*, 18.64.

18. Manfred Schulze, "Martin Luther and the Church Fathers," in *The Reception of the Church Fathers in the West: From the Carolingians to the Maurists*, vol. 2, ed. Irena Backus (Leiden: E. J. Brill, 1997), 578.

"Pelagianism" of Augustine's day is reborn. For Luther, this was the primary issue that faced the church in every age. The witness of the fathers was most useful in combating this heresy and providing the authority for opposing Roman dominance.

John Calvin's training as a humanist made him particularly sensitive to the historical connection between the apostolic and patristic roots of the church and its reform. He was well read in ancient Christian texts and convinced that the Reformation movement was in line with the doctrines of the early church. To the Roman cardinal Sadoleto he wrote:

> You teach that all which has been approved for fifteen hundred years or more, by the uniform consent of the faithful, is, by our headstrong rashness, torn up and destroyed. . . . You know . . . that our agreement with antiquity is far closer than yours, but that all we have attempted has been to renew that ancient form of the church.[19]

The true church that the apostles instituted was commensurate with the ancient form of the church exhibited in the writings of Chrysostom and Basil, among the Greek writers, and Cyprian, Ambrose, and Augustine among the Latins, which is in stark contrast to "the ruins of that church, as now surviving among yourselves."[20]

When it came to the doctrine that we are made righteous by faith and not through our works, Calvin claimed Ambrose,[21] although he more often cited Augustine. Augustine's views on sin, grace, and free will were sufficiently in harmony with Calvin's, such that the Reformer sometimes preferred to express himself with Augustine's words rather than his own. Typically, Calvin was critical of Augustine's (and Origen's) exegetical works and his use of allegory in the interpretation of Scripture. Moreover, Augustine did not sufficiently distinguish between justification and sanctification.[22] But concerning the main doctrines, Calvin saw himself as a legitimate successor of Augustine's teaching.

---

19. John Calvin, *Reply to Cardinal Sadoleto*, in *A Reformation Debate*, ed. J. C. Olin (New York: Harper, 1966), 62.

20. Ibid.

21. John Calvin, *Institutes of the Christian Religion*, ed. J. T. McNeill, trans. F. L. Battles (Philadelphia: Westminster, 1960), III.22.8.

22. Ibid., III.11.15.

At the same time, it is not accurate to say that the Reformers were merely interested in repristinating patristic theology. Nor did they see themselves as limited to the authority of the early fathers. The development of theological principles (*sola fide*, etc.), however, was believed to be an extension of apostolic teaching vindicated by the texts of the early fathers and therefore the basis of reforming catholicity. Though not equal to the authority of Scripture, the patristic testimonies demonstrated that the Reformers shared a continuity with the ancient church that Rome did not. For this reason, the Augsburg Confession in 1530 stated that "this whole cause" (*tota haec causa*) of the Reformation "is sustained by the testimonies of the Fathers."[23] Later Lutheran reformers after Trent would make the same claim. One of the authors of the Formula of Concord (1577), Andreas Musculus, wrote a theological textbook, a catechism, and a prayer book composed of citations from the fathers. Likewise, Jakob Andreae and Martin Chemnitz assembled a host of patristic quotations in reference to the doctrine of Christ, lest any Roman critic should allege that the Formula of Concord was not supported, as "the ancient pure church, its fathers and councils, have spoken."[24] When the various works of Luther and Melanchthon and other confessional documents were compiled in 1580 as the *Book of Concord*, its opening essay was a brief commentary on the three ecumenical creeds: the Apostles', the Nicene, and the Athanasian. It was an intentional move to underscore the deep conviction among evangelical theologians that the Reformation upheld and recovered the chief teachings of the ancient church.[25]

Protestant Tradition

Related to *sola fide* are two preparatory components, *solus Christus* (Christ alone) and *sola gratia* (by grace alone), that are

23. Art. XX. "This is the sum of doctrine . . . nothing which is discrepant with Scripture or with the church catholic or even with the Roman church as far as that church is known from the writings of the Fathers" (art. I.22). Augustine and Ambrose, among others, cited as defenders grace and the righteousness of faith against the merit of works.

24. Jakob Andreae and Martin Chemnitz, *Catalog of Testimonies* (1578), trans. T. Manteufel, in *Sources and Contexts in the Book of Concord*, ed. R. Kolb and J. A. Nestigen (Minneapolis: Fortress, 2001), 221.

25. R. Kolb and T. J. Wengert, eds., *The Book of Concord: The Confessions of the Evangelical Lutheran Church* (Minneapolis: Fortress, 2000), 19.

perceived (with *sola scriptura*) as the enduring bastions of evangelicalism in particular and Protestantism in general. Use of the adjective *sola* or *solus* ("alone" or "sole") excludes human participation in humankind's redemption. Although none of the sixteenth-century Reformers ever spoke of the Christian faith using these phrases together, contemporary Protestant writers, nonetheless, frequently employ them as foundational for describing an orthodox interpretation of Christianity. These terms operate much like traditions.

The principle of *sola Christus* is really the basis for the rest. The beginning and the end of the Christian faith is found in our justification in Jesus Christ alone. For Luther, Christ's death and resurrection made the gifts of grace and faith possible. The definitive text for this understanding is John 14:6: Christ is the way, the truth, and the life. "No one comes to the Father except through me." Central to the New Testament proclamation is the absolute uniqueness of Christ, also expressed in Acts 4:12: "Salvation is found in no one else." *Sola gratia* emphasizes that the God who justifies is a gracious God. Just as righteousness is made possible by Christ alone, so sinners are made righteous by God's grace alone.

Without these principles, according to various Protestant theologians, Protestantism would not be itself. The *sola* statements have served functionally, if not in name, as traditions of Protestantism, at least in Lutheran and Reformed circles. Even for those Protestants who declare that they do not acknowledge any traditions or creeds, the *solas* have acted as nothing less than theological norms for interpreting the Bible. Any mitigation of these "traditions," therefore, is tantamount to a denial of biblical faith.[26]

Of course, not all Protestants have maintained the ultimate importance of this side of Protestant tradition. A little-observed fact is that various sixteenth-century Anabaptist and free church groups, from whom the majority of evangelical churches today trace their ancestry, rejected or significantly modified Luther's

---

26. It is noteworthy that the Formula of Concord (1576), after establishing the unequivocal authority of the Bible and the importance of the Apostles', Nicene, and Athanasian creeds for doctrinal matters, makes appeal to the "Creed of our own age, called the first, unaltered Augsburg Confession [1530] . . . and likewise the Apology [of the Augsburg Confession] and the Smalcald Articles drawn up in the year 1537 and approved by subscription by the theological leaders of that time."

articulation of justification by faith. In their eyes, the teaching of *sola fide* failed to instruct believers about the need for good works. Luther's separation of justification from sanctification seemed to be a perilous move that failed to convince Christians of the centrality of holiness. Anabaptists understood the relationship between justification and sanctification in a manner that put them, ironically, closer to medieval Catholicism than to Luther.[27] These communions did not accept justification by faith as the sole criterion for measuring fidelity to the gospel. In fact, they seem to have suspected it of being an excuse for permitting a lax, comprehensive state church.[28] While later free church movements (Baptist, Pentecostal, Disciples of Christ, etc.) accept justification by faith alone as an important part of their theology, they tend to give as great an importance to the need for believers to appropriate the faith. The concern for repentance and conversion has generally led to an emphasis on faith as the human response to God's initiative.[29]

One of the historical fallacies of modern presentations of *sola fide* is that it was more or less uniformly accepted by the various reforming movements of the sixteenth century. The "traditional" aspect of *sola fide* is nowhere more apparent than in its monolithic-like appeal to represent the whole mind of Protestantism. It is especially distressing that some evangelicals demand that the *solas* are the epitome of evangelicalism and should be regarded as the only orthodoxy for evangelicals. While Luther was a dominant voice in his time, he was nevertheless one voice among many who were proclaiming the church's need for reformation. Not all reformers saw *sola fide* as being at the very heart of the gospel; nor did they all entirely embrace Luther's manner of expressing it.[30] Melanchthon, Luther's close aide and intellectual defender, was ill at ease with Luther's insistence on humanity's total passivity in God's work of justification. In distinction to the idea that a person no longer

27. David Dunbar, "Martin Luther and the Early Free Church Tradition," *Evangelical Journal of Theology* 8 (1986): 53.

28. A. N. S. Lane, *Justification by Faith in Catholic-Protestant Dialogue: An Evangelical Assessment* (Edinburgh: T & T Clark, 2002), 135.

29. See Veli-Matti Kärkkäinen, "The Apostolicity of Free Churches," *Pro Ecclesia* 10 (2001): 475–86.

30. Even Luther, in his debate with Erasmus, identified the theological center as the incarnation and suffering of the Son of God and that God is three and one. See D. Yeago, "Ecclesia Sancta, Ecclesia Peccatrix," *Pro Ecclesia* 9 (2000): 332.

acts once Christ lives in him or her, Melanchthon explained that justification must make reference to three contributing factors: the Word of God, the Holy Spirit, *and* the faculty of the human will. The latter he called the "capacity for applying oneself to grace, a way of speaking that would have not been acceptable to Luther."[31] Among those who accepted the principle of *sola fide*, there were differing applications of the concept. One of Luther's disciples, Andreas Osiander, utterly rejected the notion that justification was external to the believer, as Luther and Melanchthon had taught. Instead, Osiander claimed that saving righteousness was infused into the soul,[32] much as Augustine had claimed.

Justification and Church History

Undoubtedly, the theological concepts of unmerited grace and faith that justifies the sinner received a deserved and extensive reworking in the sixteenth and seventeenth centuries, which they had previously never received. After objecting to abuses within the sacramental structure of the medieval church, the Reformers needed to identify more precisely the necessary "hinge" on which Christian salvation swings. Part of the unspoken historical perspective behind the post-Reformation insistence that there is only one acceptable doctrinal formulation of justification by faith is the older and broader narrative that the church had lost its way about the true course of salvation until it was found by the Reformers.[33] Just as the notions of penance, tradition, and sacraments represented a series of corruptions from the simple and straightforward biblical message of the church, so the original apostolic intentions as expounded in the Pauline Epistles had become overlaid with the paraphernalia of alien teachings and practices sometime after the first century. During this time, the church allegedly imported the idea that divine forgiveness was also grounded in the righteous activity of a believer. The church's

31. Paul O'Callaghan, *Fides Christi: The Justification Debate* (Dublin: Four Courts Press, 1997), 46–47.

32. Ibid., 54.

33. For a detailed look at the pervasiveness of the church's "fall" paradigm, see D. H. Williams, *Retrieving the Tradition and Renewing Evangelicalism: A Primer for Suspicious Protestants* (Grand Rapids: Eerdmans, 1999), chap. 4.

corruption implied that its history was a history of discontinuity between the apostolic era and what followed. The only bright spot in the obfuscation of the faith's true meaning was Augustine's teaching on sin, grace, and election. His explanations on these subjects came the closest to mirroring Paul's teaching. Otherwise, the theology of the patristic and medieval periods generally suffered from distortions of biblical faith and stood in dire need of correction. It was not until the sixteenth century that the implications of Paul's teaching about justification by faith were properly interpreted and integrated into the Christian faith.

Where does such a view leave the church for its first fifteen hundred years? As A. N. S. Lane observes, the pre-Reformation church may have understood the doctrine of justifying faith, but not in terms of sixteenth-century Protestantism.[34] As long as the sixteenth-century Reformation is viewed as the restoration of apostolic Christianity and the bar by which the rest of church history is judged, then patristic and medieval Christianity are incomplete or inadequate attempts at expressing the gospel.

No less remarkable than the myth of the church's fall is its sudden recovery with Luther's discovery of the Pauline phrase "a righteousness from God" in Romans 1:17. It is debatable how much veracity should be placed on Luther's autobiographical statement of 1545 in which he recalls the events of his conversion sometime before 1518.[35] But more problematic than depicting Luther as one radically transformed from a medieval monk to an evangelical Reformer is that it fails to take seriously the purposes of the early Reformation as a restoration of catholicism.[36] It also leads to the impression that Protestant Christianity was a development independent of, or even despite, the patristic and medieval church. This view does not take into account the complexity of sources that influenced Luther's thinking on justification. Determining these sources and their precise impact on his thought continues to be a matter of scholarly investigation.[37] Still, it seems axiomatic to

34. Lane, *Justification by Faith in Catholic-Protestant Dialogue*, 146.

35. "Preface to the Complete Edition of Luther's Latin Writings" (1545), in *Martin Luther: Selections from His Writings*, ed. J. Dillenberger (Garden City, N.Y.: Doubleday, 1961), 3–12.

36. As David Yeago argues in "The Catholic Luther," in *The Catholicity of the Reformation*, ed. C. E. Braaten and R. W. Jenson (Grand Rapids: Eerdmans, 1996), 15–17.

37. See Eric Gritsch, "The Origins of the Lutheran Teaching on Justification," in *Justification by Faith*, 162–71; B. Hägglund, "The Background of Luther's Doctrine of Justification

some modern Protestant writers that the principle of justification by faith was "discovered" or "rediscovered" by the Reformers,[38] by which is meant that the important principles expounded by Paul about the truth of salvation had been overlooked or misunderstood by most of the early and medieval church.

Such a caricature is fraught with problems. Most obvious is the fact that this caricature fails to do justice to fifteen hundred years of church history. It renders the Protestant legacy ahistorical, not concerned with its place in a larger and longer Christian story, while asserting that it is the restoration of that story. This is either ignorance or arrogance, neither one befitting what Protestantism was originally intended to be.

The doctrine of justification by faith did not originate in the period of the Reformation, nor is the teaching a unique emblem of Protestantism. Evangelical scholars Timothy George and Thomas Oden have rightly observed that justification by faith was not a new teaching invented by the Reformers.[39] Apart from New Testament documents, justification by faith finds its roots in the early church. Stated positively, the exegesis of justification by faith is a catholic and pre-Reformation teaching, and the Reformers themselves found precedents for this teaching in the early fathers, even as they went in new directions with these ideas.

Paul, Justification, and the Early Tradition

While the observation that the salvific concept of justification was recognized by patristic writers is nothing new, it is not easy to find reputable studies that address this issue, and most of these (not unjustly) concern themselves with Augustine's landmark contributions. There is no question that the "later" Augustine brings the issue of justification into the mainstream of Christian doctrine, concomitantly with the notions of grace and election, permanently

---

in Late Medieval Theology," *Lutheran World* 8 (1961): 24–46; and David Steinmetz, *Luther and Staupitz: An Essay in the Intellectual Origins of the Protestant Reformation* (Durham: Duke University Press, 1980).

38. E.g., F. Hildebrandt, *Christianity according to the Wesleys* (Grand Rapids: Baker Academic, 1996), 18.

39. Timothy George, "Evangelicals and the Rule of Faith," *First Things* 106 (2000): 75; and Thomas Oden, *The Justification Reader* (Grand Rapids: Eerdmans, 2002).

putting his stamp on the theological development of the West.[40] But the status of the teaching of justification prior to Augustine seems to be largely ignored by scholars. The problem is partially due to the difficulties in locating exact theological antecedents to Augustine's mature theology, difficulties compounded by the fact that the development of a *doctrine* of justification was not a priority for early Christian thinkers. This, in turn, has fueled the conclusion that there was in the early church an overall disinterest in and misconstrual of Pauline theology until Augustine. One is reminded of T. F. Torrance's verdict against Clement and the apostolic fathers, charging them with directly contradicting Paul and promoting a theology of "works."[41] This is the implicit message in the entry "Justification" in *The Encyclopedia of the Early Church*. No writers earlier than Augustine and Pelagius are mentioned as having relevance to the patristic development of soteriology, which leaves the reader to assume that nothing of importance was written on the subject during the first four centuries of the church except, of course, for the Pauline letters.[42]

In his impressive historical survey of justification by faith, Alister McGrath dismisses what writers before Augustine had to say about the subject on the grounds that patristic Christianity suffered from an acute case of dependency on Greek philosophy rather than the Bible. McGrath concludes that in terms of a theological understanding of justification, "early theologians of the western church . . . approached their text [Latin Bible] and their subject with a set of presuppositions which owed more to the Latin language and culture than to Christianity itself."[43] Just as problematic were the Greek writers who maintained a positive estimation of the human capacity for the exercise of free will,

40. Augustine's writings overall do not present a uniform picture about sin, grace, and election, as they do not offer a uniform view about any major doctrine. A comparison of Augustine's *On Free Will*, books I–II with *On the Grace of Christ and Original Sin* and other later works demonstrates clear differences in his perspective on the relationship between human ability and God's omnipotence.

41. T. F. Torrance, *The Doctrine of Grace in the Apostolic Fathers* (Edinburgh: Oliver & Boyd, 1948), 44–45.

42. *The Encyclopedia of Early Christianity*, s.v. "Justification," acknowledges Origen's commentary on Romans but states that "the only patristic author who seems to appreciate the distinctively Pauline teaching was Augustine."

43. Alister McGrath, *Iustitia Dei: A History of the Christian Doctrine of Justification*, 2 vols. (Cambridge: Cambridge University Press, 1986), 1.15.

with which they associated the importance of obedience and of achieving purity. It is no wonder, therefore, that writers before Augustine all sound like Pelagians.

But was the early church before Augustine so ignorant of Paul's Epistles and misguided as to their teaching? Several indications demonstrate that the concept of justifying faith was initially developed in the patristic era and well before the Pelagian controversy broke out (i.e., c. 411–12).

Early church historians generally agree that the theological emphases during the patristic era were centered around ontological issues of the divine nature as it relates to a trinitarian understanding of God and the being and work of Christ as God incarnate. As the early church sought to define its identity in light of its Jewish roots and as the tensions between Jewish Christians and Gentile Christians continued well into the second century, debate about the relationship between law and gospel often impinged on the Christian idea of salvation.

Against the perceived imbalances among certain Jewish Christians, Polycarp's letter to the Smyrnaeans cites Ephesians 2:8: "By grace you have been saved, through faith—and this not from yourselves, it is the gift of God—not by works, so that no one can boast." Polycarp may have seen in his own mid-second century situation a continuation of the struggle Paul waged against a Jewish-Christian doctrine of legalism, which he too wished to correct as inconsistent with the gospel. The letters of Ignatius and the *Epistle of Barnabas* clearly show that severe conflicts took place between Christians and Jewish Christians over the relevance of the law in the interpretation of the Christian message. The extremes of judaizing Christians who mandated a literal reading of the Mosaic covenant, on the one hand, and Marcion's complete rejection of the historical relevance of the Old Testament for Christianity, on the other hand, were already coming into expression by this time. But concern with such extremes was not the sole occasion for echoing Pauline theology. The late-first-century letter known as *1 Clement* contains almost solely quotations from the Hebrew Bible yet exhibits a predominance of Pauline themes, such as frequent reference to believers as God's elect, the use of doxologies, and contentions that God's faithful are made just by faith.[44]

44. See *1 Clement* 2.5; 32.4; 58.3.

Also among the Apostolic Fathers corpus, the anonymous *Epistle to Diognetus,* written about the same time as Polycarp's letter, manifests theological sensitivity to the relationship between the sinfulness and powerlessness of the human condition before God and our need for the righteousness of God. This text contains no direct quotations from the Pauline Epistles. Still, the writer speaks plainly of an inability to enter the kingdom of God according to one's own worthiness or goodness. Hope of salvation lies only in the saving power of God, which was demonstrated by the ransoming of his righteous Son for humanity's unrighteousness.

> In whom was it possible for us, the lawless and ungodly, to be justified, except in the Son of God alone? O sweet exchange, O the incomprehensible work of God, O the unexpected blessings, that the sinfulness of many should be hidden in one righteous man, while the righteousness of one should justify many sinners![45]

None of these instances reveals the initial expounding of a doctrine of justification by faith. It is accurate to say only that there are occasional moments of direct reflection on Pauline theology during the first three centuries, and when these instances do occur, there is often recognition that the righteous are made righteous by faith. Of course, one can also find very un-Pauline perspectives, such as the injunction in the *Didache* (19:10) for one to work to ransom one's sins (though the writer is not propounding a soteriology). The *Shepherd of Hermas,* likewise, presents the Christian faith in terms that demonstrate almost a complete ignorance of God's gracious act of redemption in Christ.[46] Despite these cases, however, there is no need to think that patristic writers had become so philosophically and culturally intoxicated that they were no longer concerned with establishing clarity regarding the way of salvation based on Scripture and the church's tradition.

The biblical commentaries written by Origen of Alexandria in the middle of the third century reveal what early Greek Christianity thought of the books of Romans and Ephesians. Clement of Alexandria is said to have made brief comments on Paul's

---

45. *Epistle to Diognetus* 9.4–5.

46. *Shepherd, Vision* 2.2: "If this sin is recorded against me, how can I be saved? Or how will I propitiate God for my conscious sins?" Cf. *Shepherd, Vision* 3.10; and *Mandate* 3.28.

Epistles,[47] but other than a few fragments, this work is not extant. Even so, Origen's efforts represent the first known large-scale commentary on select Pauline letters among Latin or Greek writers. His work demonstrates clearly that he insisted on the absolute necessity of faith and good works; the two are organically linked in such a way that Origen rarely articulates the one without the other. In his commentary on Romans, Origen presents faith as a truly personal relationship with Christ grounded solely on receiving faith, just as it had happened for the thief on the cross or the woman who was a sinner (Luke 7). At the same time, he safeguards the idea from any approach that interprets God's justifying faith as an excuse for the absence of pursuing personal righteousness. Origen was chiefly concerned about those who used faith to escape moral culpability because their actions were predetermined by God or the stars or because their nature had preordained them to a course of action.[48] Belief that does not yield the fruit of good works is therefore in vain. The efficacy of saving faith, as Paul expresses it in unqualified and all-embracing terms, appears in Origen, though in brief and restricted ways.

Thanks to the postmortem popularity of Origen in the later fourth and early fifth century, Greek writers, most notably John Chrysostom, similarly espoused the coordinating efforts of divine grace and human response.[49] Furthermore, the translation of many of Origen's works by Rufinus, Jerome, and others meant that the commentary on Romans was available to Latin readers and would have its most enduring effect in the West. Pelagius certainly knew of it and used it. A convincing case has also been made by the late C. P. Bammel that Augustine was indebted to Origen's commentary as the African

47. The work is called *Hypotyposes* by Eusebius of Caesarea, *HE* VI.14, 1.

48. Origen, *Commentary on Romans* II.4, 7

49. E.g., John Chrysostom, *Homily on the Gospel of Matthew* 82. "From this we learn an important doctrine, that people's good will is not enough if they are not in receipt of grace from on high, and correlatively that we profit nothing from grace from on high if good will is lacking. Both these truths Judas and Peter demonstrate: though one enjoyed much assistance, it did him no good because he lacked good will and contributed nothing of his own, whereas the latter, though full of good will, came to grief because he received no assistance. Virtue, you see, is woven from these two things. Hence I urge you not to leave it all up to God and fall asleep, nor in a flurry of zeal to think you achieve the whole thing by your own efforts. In fact, God does not want us to be lethargic—hence his not doing everything himself; nor to be presumptuous—hence his not leaving it all up to us; instead, he removed the harmful element in each option, and left to us the beneficial part."

bishop struggled with the Pauline emphasis on justification by faith and the necessity of good works after baptism.[50]

Justification in the Fourth Century

In the Latin literature, it was not until the mid-fourth century with the commentaries on Galatians, Ephesians, and Titus by Marius Victorinus that Western theology began to make a more thorough inquiry into the implications of Pauline theology. One of the few scholarly examinations of the early Latin patristic use of Paul's thought focused on these commentaries, and results of this work make it clear that Victorinus taught salvation by grace through faith,[51] though he does not seek to investigate beyond the Pauline wording. We are freed from our sins by belief in Christ, but good works are expected to follow this forgiveness in a reciprocal fashion.

While Victorinus may have produced the first exegetical treatments of the Pauline Epistles, he was not the first to integrate the teaching of justification by faith into Christian theology. Virtually ignored among the treatments of early Christian thought is Hilary of Poitiers, a bishop and theologian whose contributions were seminal for the establishment of trinitarian and christological theology in the West before Augustine. But just as noteworthy was Hilary's commentary on the Gospel of Matthew. This is a remarkable work in several ways, not least in that it is the first Latin biblical commentary to be preserved almost completely intact.[52] It also reveals the prominence of the Pauline theme of justifying faith a half century before Augustine. Given the centrality of justifying faith in the commentary, it is fitting that we examine it more closely.

Twenty occurrences of the phrase "justification by faith" are mentioned throughout the thirty-three-chapter work, demonstrating its importance in Hilary's understanding of the gospel. Clearly, Hilary's

50. C. P. Bammel, "Justification by Faith in Augustine and Origen," *Journal of Ecclesiastical History* 47 (1996): 223–35.

51. Robert Eno, "Some Patristic Views on the Relationship of Faith and Works in Justification," *Recherches Augustiniennes* 19 (1984): 3–27. A shorter version of the same title is found in Anderson, *Justification by Faith*, 111–30.

52. Jean Doignon produced a new critical edition for the commentary in 1978 (*Sources chrétiennes*, vols. 254, 258). The first English translation of the work will appear in the near future in the Fathers of the Church series.

interest involves much more than mere restatements of Pauline passages. The fact that this author, writing a commentary on Matthew, utilizes Paul's language and concepts so frequently demonstrates that they are for him an indispensable factor in achieving an adequate understanding of how a sinner is made righteous.

Fundamental to Hilary's description of the message of salvation is the idea that the bonds of the law, chained by its acknowledgment of sin, are loosed "through an understanding of evangelical freedom."[53] Even though the same law proclaimed Christ and his coming (cf. Luke 24:44–47) and was established for the realization of the need for faith (XVI.3), it became a liability when used as an end in itself, effectively preventing many Jews from appropriating Christ. The problem with trying to keep the law is that one is not able to follow it and accept God's justifying grace. By not having faith, those who follow the law lose what they have of the law (XIII.2). Hilary often contrasts the legalism of unbelief and unworthiness with salvific faith. The former is a salvation of works that leads to unbelief and even animosity toward faith, whereas those who have no achievement to their credit are prepared to realize that "salvation is entirely by faith" (XI.10).[54]

The model of obedience for the Jews was Abraham, who was worthy as one justified by faith, so that "through faith believers are the descendants of Abraham" (II.3). Of course, if justice had come from the law, forgiveness through grace would not have been necessary (IX.2). Only an abuse of the law, as seen in the Pharisees, brings about an opposition to the necessity of faith. Before and after the coming of Christ, the means of righteousness was the same: that which comes only "through grace of the gospel's justification" (XXVII.7). This fact was vividly demonstrated, just as Origen had acknowledged, by the thief on the cross who was saved only by justification by faith. Salvation lies only in the goodness of God, a goodness that Hilary calls "the perfect gift" (XII.5; XIII.2): We are

53. Hilary, *On Matthew* XI.2. This is more than a passing theme for Hilary. Cf. XI.8 ("freedom of life in Christ"), XIX.10 ("freedom of the gospel"), and XXX.11 ("liberty of the gospel").

54. The withered fig tree in Matt. 21 is said to be a figure of the chief priests and Pharisees who "have not been justified by faith, nor have they returned through repentance to salvation" (ibid., XXI.14). The pagans, on the other hand, are justified by the entry of salvation and it is "for their sakes [the Lord] is come" (ibid., XXI.2). Not all is lost for the Jews, however, since "just as some believed through the apostles, so it is through Elijah that others will believe and be justified by faith" (ibid., XXVI.5).

"made alive through the grace of the Spirit whose gift comes . . . through faith" (XV.10).

The parable of the workers in the vineyard illustrates for Hilary that salvation is completely God's gift (Matt. 20:1–16). The workers hired at the eleventh hour of the day received the same wages as those hired in the morning. The remuneration for the former demonstrates that it was not based on the merit of their labor. Rather, "God has freely granted his grace to all through justification by faith" (XX.7). This was the only means, Hilary says, by which the pagans (Gentiles) were saved. They were the last ones "hired" by the owner of the vineyard yet the first to receive remuneration.

> When it began to get late, the workers of the evening hour were the first to obtain the payment of the resurrection determined for an entire day's work. The resurrection is in no way based on the payment, because it was owed for work rendered, but God has freely granted his grace to everyone by the justification of faith. . . . God bestows the gift of grace by faith on those who believe, either first or last."[55]

Hilary was the first Christian theologian to formulate explicitly what Paul left implicit by referring to God's work of grace as *fides sola iustificat*: Because "faith alone justifies . . . publicans and prostitutes will be first in the kingdom of heaven" (XXI.14). Yet it was not his intention to elaborate on an overall scheme of salvation but to explain how the pagans came to share legitimately in the covenant originally given only to Israel.

While Hilary does not articulate a concept of original sin, he anticipates the mature views of Augustine through his reading of Paul. He declares that all humanity is implicated in Adam's downfall, that no person is without sin and no one by his own merits can free himself from that sin. Because of the sin of one, the sentence of condemnation is passed on all.[56] Not only does he espouse this doctrine, but he also comes as close as any writer before Augustine to formulating the term "original sin."

> When therefore, we are renewed in the laver of baptism through the power of the Word, we are separated from the sin and source of our

---

55. Ibid., XX.7. In this one section, Hilary emphasizes three times the unmerited gift of grace by the justification of faith.

56. Ibid., XVIII.6; Augustine, *The Trinity* VI.21.

origin [*ab originis nostrae peccatis atque auctoribus*], and when we have endured a sort of excision from the sword of God, we differ from the dispositions of our father and mother [e.g., Adam and Eve].[57]

Only by regeneration does the free gift of God avail the human condition. Moreover, the grace by which a believer is transformed is God's spontaneous, unconditional, and free gift. Despite the fact that sin entered the world through one man, the gift of grace of the one Man, Jesus Christ, brings forgiveness. Like his Latin predecessors, however, Hilary does not view human nature as completely helpless and moribund in the exercise of its moral will. God authorized humanity to exercise free will in the practice of good or evil as well as in responding freely to the gospel.

The Generation of St. Paul

The importance of Pauline theology in Hilary's writing was not an isolated case. There is a strong likelihood that Hilary's commentary sparked or fueled the revival of Pauline studies in the West during the last decades of the fourth century and the early fifth century. Hilary's writings appear to have been copied and made widely available soon after his death,[58] and within a decade, a common interest in Pauline texts and themes is evident among such widely divergent thinkers as Augustine, Tyconius (a North African Donatist who was well known to Augustine), the monk Pelagius, and Priscillian of Barcelona, a reputed neo-Manichaean. This revival of Pauline biblical texts within the Latin church was dubbed by Peter Brown as the generation of St. Paul.[59] Correspondingly, the second half of the fourth century saw a rapid increase in the number of biblical commentaries published in the West. Such commentaries became the all-important medium of transmitting theology, which

57. Hilary, *On Matthew* X 24.
58. C. Kannengiesser, "L'Héritage d'Hilaire de Poitiers," *Recherches de science religieuse* 56 (1968). 435–56; and P. Smulders, "Remarks on the Manuscript Tradition of the *De Trinitate* of Saint Hilary of Poitiers," *Texte und Untersuchungen* 78 (1961): 129–38. Already by 430, the same year Augustine died, a dossier or florilegium of Hilarian texts was circulating in the West and was being used by Arnobius the Younger, Leo of Rome, John Cassian, and Celestine of Rome.
59. Peter Brown, *Augustine: A Biography* (Berkeley: University of California Press, 1967), 151.

had previously been conveyed mainly by polemical treatises. Given the fact that Hilary's trinitarian and christological theology is often cited by later writers, it stands to reason that Hilary's Matthew commentary would have exerted no less influence on subsequent Latin literature.[60]

Augustine's experiences and theology show that he was a benefactor of the renewed interest in Paul's letters and that he stood in a succession of writers who benefited from the repercussions of Pauline theology shaping Latin hermeneutics. In addition to the works of Marius Victorinus, those of the Italian writer called "Ambrosiaster" by modern scholars suggest that the renewed interest in Pauline theology was already underway by the late 370s.[61] The latter's complete set of commentaries on the Pauline Epistles reveals the exegetical enthusiasm present at the time, as do Jerome's commentaries on Galatians, Ephesians, and Philemon. The tight focus on justifying faith is not exhibited in these writings to the same degree as in Hilary's commentary, but the emphasis on unmerited grace is certainly present.

Pelagius, writing on the same scale as Ambrosiaster and perhaps in opposition to his conclusions, published brief commentaries on all Paul's letters.[62] During the late fourth century, Augustine and Pelagius were similar in juxtaposing faith and good works. Indeed, Augustine treated Pelagius with deference and with an irenic spirit before A.D. 411–12. Of course, Pelagius had not denied the central place of grace but had affirmed the perseverance of *natural* grace, which meant that one did not have to sin. Augustine evolved in ways that set him apart from his earlier perspectives by stressing (1) the inability of the "natural man" to choose and do the good, and (2) God's sovereignty and his affirmation of the absolute priority of grace. In no way can God's purposes of redemption be thwarted or assisted by human choices—an axiom that Luther later espoused as central to his theology. A sinner is completely justified by faith

60. P. Smulders, "Hilarius van Poitiers als Exegeet van Mattheüs" (Hilary of Poitiers as an Exegete of St. Matthew), *Bijdragen* 44 (1983): 75.

61. In the 370s, Ambrosiaster emphasized the effect of original sin inherited by all humanity. We thus all sinned en masse in Adam and stand guilty before God. See A. Pollastri, *Ambrosiaster: Commento alla Lettera ai Romani* (Aquileia: L. U. Japadre, 1996), 106–15.

62. A. Souter, "The Earliest Latin Commentaries on the Epistles of St. Paul," *Texts and Studies* 9 (1926): 39–95; *Patrologiae cursus completus, series latina, supplementum* I.1110–374; and T. De Bruyn, *Pelagius's Commentary on St Paul's Epistle to the Romans* (Oxford: Clarendon, 1993).

because nothing on the part of a sinner can promote or stall God's salvific action on his behalf. Put in this way, one may say that Augustine was not propounding a doctrine of soteriology as much as he was defending a theology proper to the statement "I believe in God the Father Almighty."

Justifying Faith within the Tradition

It should go without saying that the theologians of the early church did not articulate soteriology in the same way as the sixteenth-century Reformers, nor should we expect them to have done so. It is entirely anachronistic to judge the merits of the former solely in light of the latter. Of course, the early fathers did not directly address many of the issues that would vex theologians a millennium later. While patristic texts used a certain form of words such as "faith alone" or "grace alone," it is quite another matter to show that the meaning of the one coincides with the other.

Allowing it to speak on its own terms, early Christian thought calls us to reconsider the divine richness out of which emerged Christian perspectives of salvation in general and justification in particular, a point that is emphatically reiterated by the vast knowledge and use of the early fathers by the majority of the Reformers.[63] Instead of mitigating the contributions of the early church, we may rather observe the ways in which the early church serves to balance the Protestant tradition of declaring that justification is only an alien or external righteousness or that justification must be imputed in order to have saving efficacy. On this point, Erasmus complained to Luther that his reforms too easily rejected ancient theologians' interpretation of the Bible.

> And even though Christ's Spirit might permit His people to be in error over an unimportant question on which man's salvation does not depend, how credible is it that He should have overlooked error

63. The years between 1527 and 1565—the time before the Council of Trent and when Protestantism became much more theologically defensive—saw the publication of twenty-three anthologies of patristic writings partly or totally devoted to the doctrine of justification. A. N. S. Lane, "Justification in Sixteenth-Century Patristic Anthologies," in *Auctoritas Patrum: Contributions on the Reception of the Church Fathers in the Fifteenth and Sixteenth Century,* ed. L. Grane, A. Schindler, and M. Wriedt, 69–95 (Mainz: Philipp von Zabern, 1993).

in His Church for more than thirteen hundred years, and have found not a single one of those saintly people worthy of being inspired with what my opponents [Luther and his followers] claim is the most important teaching of the entire gospel?[64]

In general, the fathers maintained the free and unmerited character of God's grace toward us, expressing it sometimes in the terms of justification by faith, although they saw ongoing justification in a different light.[65] Making firm differentiations between justification and sanctification was not the essence of doctrinal discourse for them. More pertinent to the early church's thinking as it concerned faith and justification was how a believer was purified. Ultimately, salvation was a spirituality that stressed the goal of the Christian life as the purification of the soul, in accordance with the principles implied in Titus 2:11–14. As we have seen, a definitive conversion was important, but the majority of early fathers stressed that God's work in the life of a Christian was more a process than a point. Only through purification could a believer hope to apprehend God in this life and the next. Whereas later theology assigned purification to the sanctification of a believer, patristic theology made no functional difference between the two. Purification and justification are joint acts of the Spirit, operating in the life of a believer and enabling him or her to "see" God.

Unlike the trivial sort of gospel preaching that one encounters in too many churches today where the goal of "accepting" Christ is so that one will go to heaven, the early fathers believed that God's salvation through the life, death, and resurrection of Christ meant providing a believer with the means to perceive God and thereby share in his divine life. That is, salvation was supposed to culminate in divine *theosis* or deification—becoming transformed according to God—a seminal part of the teaching of early fathers such as Irenaeus, Athanasius, and Gregory of Nyssa. The point is that faith is a divine work of salvation "in us" as well as "for us" in order to change us, that we may behold God. Protestants seeking to learn about the entire heritage of their faith should ponder seriously the way in which the earlier centuries of the Christian story

64. Erasmus, *De Libero arbitrio diatribe*, in *Collected Works of Erasmus*, ed. C. Trinkus, trans. P. Macardle and C. H. Miller (Toronto: University of Toronto Press, 1999), 20.
65. R. B. Eno, "Some Patristic Views on the Relationship of Faith and Works in Justification," in *Justification by Faith*, 111–30.

and other parts of the Christian family, such as Eastern Orthodox, have expressed the wonder of God's salvation.

Various patristic witnesses to Scripture do not always use Pauline theology as the grid by which all other scriptural testimonies are evaluated, nor do they share Luther's idea of a canon within a canon. Rather, one finds among the developing views of soteriology in early Christianity that justification is integral to the whole work of the Trinity that flows out of the life of God, manifested in a believer by faith and good works leading toward virtue. However we choose to define the righteousness of God that comes by faith, this doctrine must be indissolubly linked to the doctrine of the Trinity, for the righteousness of God—a central point in the justification event—cannot be understood apart from the life of the Triune God.[66]

"The Joint Declaration on the Doctrine of Justification" signed by Roman Catholic and Lutheran representatives more accurately reflects the kind of emphasis found in the early church. It states in paragraph 15:

> In faith we together hold the conviction that justification is the work of the triune God. The Father sent his Son into the world to save sinners. The foundation and presupposition of justification is the incarnation, death and resurrection of Christ. Justification thus means that Christ himself is our righteousness, in which we share through the Holy Spirit in accord with the will of the Father.

As per the "Joint Declaration," justification is not the supreme touchstone of Christian doctrine. It asserts, on the contrary, that justification must be integrated within the church's "rule of faith," which is centered on the Triune God and the incarnation.[67] Not making the doctrine of justification the supreme touchstone does not undermine its theological efficacy and importance for evangelicalism and Protestantism. To place it within the larger scheme of the Christian

---

66. What makes Jüngel's book more compelling than other twentieth-century Protestant defenses of justification is that he shows how a trinitarian conception is integral to it, though only a few pages are spent on this important connection (*Justification*, 82–85). The author vitiates the theological benefit accrued by this point when he demands simultaneously that justification hold the absolutely privileged position by which all other Christian doctrines are to be judged (47).

67. Avery Dulles, "Two Languages of Salvation: The Lutheran-Catholic Joint Declaration," *First Things* 98 (1999): 28.

story and message is to rediscover how Christ as "God with us," not a scheme of soteriology, is the basis of our salvation.

The Wholeness of the Biblical Testimony

It is not extraordinary that the patristic interpreters of Scripture did not use Pauline theology as the template by which all other scriptural testimonies were understood. In various parts of the New Testament corpus, the gospel is expressed in completely different terms. While there is a discernible unity to the Gospels and the Epistles, there is not the uniformity of proclamation that the platform of *sola fide* would suggest. The fact that justification is rarely mentioned outside of Romans and Galatians (cf. 1 Cor. 6:11; Titus 3:7) does little to support the use of justification as *the* biblical criterion. Above all, when Paul does single out some doctrines (plural) "as of first importance" (1 Cor. 15:3), he focuses on the death and resurrection of Christ, as also seen in the common confession (1 Tim. 3:16). It is noteworthy that these do not include justification by faith.[68] The New Testament cannot and should not be reduced to the teaching of justification by faith alone.

To insist that justification by faith is the pivotal point around which the biblical message turns necessitates the acknowledgment of a doctrinal canon (justification principle) within the canon (Scripture). This is what Luther did and what some contemporary Protestant theologians are doing,[69] but very few evangelicals are willing to go this far formally and materially when it comes to treating Scripture. Among Lutherans, discussion continues about how the doctrine of justification ought not stand alone from the totality of the rest of Scripture and the trinitarian and christological truths of the historic faith.[70]

Ancient notions of God's grace and human ability were derived from a governing perspective of the Bible's wholeness. Basic to

68. Lane, *Justification by Faith in Catholic-Protestant Dialogue*, 143–44.

69. McGrath writes that "there never was, and there never can be, any true Christian church without the doctrine of justification" (as presented by Luther) (McGrath, *Iustitia Dei*, 1.1.

70. Eero Huovinen, "How Do We Continue? The Ecumenical Commitments and Possibilities of the *Joint Declaration on the Doctrine of Justification*," *Pro Ecclesia* 11 (2001): 170. Huovinen is the bishop of Helsinki, Evangelical Lutheran Church of Finland.

this hermeneutical perspective was that any one text of Scripture had to be interpreted in light of all of Scripture, both Old and New Testaments. There was nothing accidental about this perspective. It emerged out of three centuries of doubt about and dispute over the relevance of various biblical texts among the new people of God. Scripture shares an inner coherence and design because of its divine origins, which means that the act of interpretation is in reality a task of unveiling and clarifying the pattern of truths already present in the structure. A theology gained from one text can and should inform the construal of other texts. It was automatic, therefore, for patristic writers to find Pauline perspectives in their reading of the gospel and vice versa.[71] They would not have shared the antagonistic exegesis of the early twentieth-century New Testament scholars who pitted Matthew's Jewish rendering of the gospel against the apostle to the Gentiles. For Hilary, as we have seen, the Gospel of Matthew itself taught and illustrated the teaching of justification by faith. He was not blind to the differences that existed between Pauline and Matthean texts, but, like earlier Latin commentators, he read them as parts of the same divine continuum, and they therefore shared the same purposes.

This holistic approach to the Bible is also related to a basic conviction of the early church that the work of justification is integral to the whole work of the Trinity, from whom flows the life of God, experienced by a believer through faith and in good works leading toward virtue. Any theory of salvation is only as potent as its theory about the God who provides it. For this reason, Karl Barth refused to accept the doctrine of justification by faith as, in Luther's words, "the teacher, chief, lord, rule and judge over all other doctrines" of the evangelical message. While the necessity and importance of the particular function of the justification article cannot be denied, it is just that: a particular aspect of the Christian message of reconciliation. It is not *the* theological truth on which everything else is based. Barth rightly contended that this doctrine had not always been *the* Word of the gospel and that it would be "an act of narrowing and unjust exclusiveness" in the church's theological history were we to treat it as such.[72] Rather, the being and activity of Jesus

71. E.g., Origen, *Commentarii in evangelium Joannis* I.5, 10; I.4, 23; II.9, 21; and idem, *Commentarium series in evangelium Matthaei* X.2, 5, 9; XI.3.

72. Karl Barth, *Christian Dogmatics* (Edinburgh: T & T Clark, 1936), IV/1.523.

Christ for us are the center of Christian theology and provide cohesiveness for drawing all its doctrinal aspects together.[73] We would expect Barth to say this, of course, but his point about the priority of God's revelation of himself is nevertheless well taken. The basis and culmination of the doctrine of justification are in the church's confession of the life of God imparted to us in Christ.

In the end, skepticism about the value of saving faith and unmerited grace in the patristic period is not warranted. Virtually every early church writer would have wholeheartedly agreed with Paul's words: "Therefore, if anyone is in Christ, he is a new creature; the old has gone, the new has come! All this is from God, who reconciled us to himself through Christ" (2 Cor. 5:17–18). It was all but universally accepted that the work of salvation is completely God's work on our behalf. We are not saved by our good deeds. Part of the corrective that may be necessary as contemporary Protestantism seeks to understand itself in light of the entire inheritance of the historic faith is that we must see that the Reformation in the West, valuable as it was, obscured earlier voices that also spoke for orthodoxy and the church, voices that can again contribute to discussions about the theological roots of justification by faith.

The Protestant principles of *sola scriptura* and *sola fide* do not themselves constitute orthodox Christianity, nor do they constitute the very heart of the historic Christian faith. These were originally intended to subsist under the umbrella of the ancient tradition. The purpose here is not to mitigate their place or force within Protestant Christianity; it is to insist that the proper way to assess their value is to situate them within the broader contours of catholicity. The ancient rule of the church's faith is better suited to designate the central identity of historic Christianity than the Protestant *solas*, just as *the* tradition remains the foundation on which these later Protestant "traditions" build.

---

73. Ibid., IV/1.527–28.

GLIMPSES AT THE RESOURCES
OF THE ANCIENT TRADITION

Those who study and translate the Fathers are giving up the best years of their lives . . . to the most laborious drudgery and most thankless of all tasks.

> Thomas Mozley (John Henry Newman's brother-in-law),
> *Reminiscences Chiefly of Oriel College
> and the Oxford Movement* (1882)

I HAVE OFTEN A strange feeling," the Greek Orthodox theologian George Florovsky once wrote, "when I read the ancient classics of Christian theology, the fathers of the church, I find them more relevant to the troubles and problems of my own time than the production of modern theologians."[1] Within his Greek Orthodoxy, Florovsky had been exposed to the early fathers and their perennial relevance, but this is not the case with many

1. George Florovsky, *Bible, Church, Tradition: An Eastern Orthodox View* (Belmont, Mass.: Nordland, 1972), 16.

church families of Protestantism. Now that previous chapters have hopefully cleared some obstacles that have prevented evangelicals from appropriating the early tradition as a vital and necessary resource for the reconstruction of an integral Christian faith, this chapter looks at several concrete examples of the tradition in action. It is reasonable to ask, once we have considered some problems associated with the tradition in relation to Scripture and the authorial doctrines of *sola scriptura* and *sola fide,* where does one turn to see and hear the tradition functioning within the early church?

The tradition is a composite and constructed entity that has a history. No ideal of the tradition exists apart from its various manifestations in specific times and places. Yet the tradition cannot be determined by a single exhibit. Functioning dynamically as well as possessing a content, it is found within a series of defining moments within the life of the church. These defining moments are found in several specific contexts to which one can point and describe. Collectively they reveal the substance of the church's faith as it unfolds and is defined. While textbooks of Christian history often look to the great creeds as the pinnacles of defining the Christian faith, it is a woefully inadequate approach to church history simply because the tradition constitutes a number of diverse expressions. The great creeds are but one aspect of the church's tradition.

No one of the major creeds of the early church was meant to be comprehensive in its teaching, nor was any one of them meant to stand alone, as if it were the final word on the subject of Christian faith. My evangelical friends who complain that the ancient creeds do not say enough about Christ's incarnation and redemption as revealed in the Gospels make a valid point. Creeds are by no means all-inclusive in their teaching. The major creeds were emblematic of Christian teaching and therefore only representative of what faithful Christians believe. The fact that the Nicene Creed and the Apostles' Creed later appear in church liturgies as condensed doctrinal statements demonstrates their emblematic function. They were not totalizing formulas for calculating the entire mystery of Christian identity.

We must look, instead, to an assortment of witnesses, which themselves present a unified (not a uniform) picture of the church's professed faith. Following the lead of Irenaeus, we see that the church's tradition is like a set of deposits in the treasury of the church. This last chapter, therefore, focuses on specific "deposits" of the tradition as they were made within various contexts of the ancient church's faith. A multitude of ancient witnesses are still extant that show us how the tradition was at work in the life of the church. Sorting these witnesses into neat categories risks creating artificial groupings that did not exist in any formal sense. Nevertheless, varied kinds of patristic evidence can be grouped into thematic families without losing the interrelated unity. What follows are mere glimpses into the available evidence that show where and how the tradition was incarnated. In this limited sampling of texts, pilgrims will find direction to the marvelous treasure trove of resources for the Christian journey.[2]

Professions of Faith

Contrary to the view that confessions or creeds are artificial elements that Christians used (and still use) as substitutes for a vibrant and personal faith, they originated in the very life of the church. Whether immediately preceding baptism, preparing candidates for baptism, or providing a general course of right teaching, "professions of the faith" emerged from the living activities of early Christian communities. This is what Florovsky means when he declares that we ought to "preach the creeds." The creeds have value for the church today because they emerged from the message of Scripture and historic doctrine.

Another perceived problem with confessional forms of faith is that they may insinuate a kind of legalist Christianity that some denominations associate with fundamentalism. In this case, a creed is perceived as a legislated statement of power used for manipulating the faithful. Resorting to a creed magnifies the authority of the institution and stifles individual expression and response. Something like credal paranoia afflicts a large number of Protestants who loathe contemporary statements of faith and thereby have little use for ancient ones. This is particularly true

---

2. Besides the texts introduced in this chapter, see the forthcoming sourcebook published by Baker Academic for a more extensive listing of patristic witnesses.

for many in Baptist circles. At best, creeds are tolerated as corporate expressions, but they are not seen as useful for informing a deep personal faith.

When it comes to conciliar statements of faith (creeds issued at councils), an assembly of bishops did not itself make for sound Christian doctrine. Nor could episcopal opinion stand independently on its own merits. Credal statements had to represent the common mind of the church. If they did not, they would not have been accepted and employed by the larger body of believing Christians. As Charles Williams once said of the Christian faith encapsulated in the Nicene Creed, "It had become a Creed, and it remained a Gospel."[3]

Creeds were not a mere ideal scarcely realized in practice. The vigilance of bishops to guard orthodox faith when attending councils is exemplified in Eusebius of Caesarea's letter to his congregation. He explains to them, just after he had reluctantly subscribed to the Nicene Creed, that he would never have agreed to a statement that contradicted the faith of the Caesarean church. Making every inquiry, Eusebius says, into the terminology and intent of the creed's wording, "it appeared to us to coincide with what we ourselves have professed in the faith which we have previously declared."[4] Fortunately for us, Eusebius actually quotes both his church creed and the Nicene Creed. It has been suggested that the similarities between the two have to do with the Nicene Creed's reliance on the Caesarean creed, though it is more likely that the Nicene Creed drew from the Jerusalem creed or something much like it. While no document contains the creed of the Jerusalem church, its formula of faith has been culled from *The Catechetical Addresses* of Cyril of Jerusalem. In any case, the conciliar statement drew from the earlier thought and terminology of the church's faith. English translations of the three Greek creeds follow.

The Caesarean Creed
We believe in One God, Father Almighty, Maker of all things visible and invisible;

3. Charles Williams, *The Descent of the Dove: A Short History of the Holy Spirit in the Church* (Grand Rapids: Eerdmans, 1939), 49.
4. Quoted in J. Stevenson, ed., *A New Eusebius: Documents Illustrating the History of the Church to AD 337* (London: SPCK, 1987), 347.

And in one Lord Jesus Christ, the Word of God, God from God, Light from Light, Life from Life, Only-begotten Son, first-born of creation, begotten of the Father before all ages, by whom all things were made; who for our salvation was incarnate, and lived among men, and suffered, and rose again on the third day, and ascended to the Father, and will come again in glory to judge the living and the dead.

And in one Holy Spirit.

The Nicene Creed

We believe in one God, the Father, almighty, maker of all things visible and invisible;

And in one Lord Jesus Christ, the son of God, begotten from the Father, only-begotten, that is, from the substance of the Father, God from God, light from light, true God from true God, begotten not made, of one substance from the Father, through Whom all things came into being, things in heaven and things on earth, who because of us men and because of our salvation came down and became incarnate, becoming man, suffered and rose again on the third day, ascended to the heavens, will come to judge the living and the dead;

And in the Holy Spirit.[5]

The Jerusalem Creed

We believe in one God, the Father Almighty, maker of heaven and earth, of all things visible and invisible;

And in one Lord Jesus Christ, the only-begotten Son of God, who was begotten of the Father as true God, only-begotten before all ages, by whom all things were made; who appeared in the flesh, and became man; who was crucified and buried and rose again from the dead on the third day, and ascended to heaven, and sat down on the right hand of the Father, and will come again in glory to judge the living and the dead, of whose kingdom there will be no end;

And in one Holy Spirit, the Paraclete, who spoke in the prophets, and in one baptism of repentence for the remission of sins; and in

5. One anathema is attached to the creed: "But as for those who say, there was when he was not, and, before being born he was not, and he came into existence out of nothing, or who assert that the son of God is a different hypostasis or substance, or is subject to change or alteration—-these the Catholic and Apostolic Church anathematizes."

one holy catholic church, and in the resurrection of the flesh, and in the life everlasting.[6]

One early fifth-century definition of the original Greek word for creed, *symbolum*, was "token" or "sign."[7] In other words, the creed was a designated symbol for a fuller and wider description of the church's faith, from which it stemmed. It stood for the *consensus fidelium* (a consensus of the faithful), a kind of verbal extension of the believing communities. It could be expressed through a council of bishops, in a manual of discipleship, or in a baptismal confession, but it was not something foisted upon the churches as a foreign object. Creeds were confessions of faith, not mere political statements of will. Of course, a party could hide its agenda within the shadow of a creed, substituting piety for power. Church history is unfortunately filled with such abuses of creeds. But on the whole, conciliar professions were the amalgam of theological and historical precursors (as one finds in baptismal creeds), and therefore their veracity was validated by upholding them. Just as local confessions and the rule of faith were designed with the purpose of determining sound belief, conciliar creeds were also framed with this end in view. Both local and conciliar standards of faith commonly shared the idea of excluding error as a means of maintaining theological purity within the church.

Ancient creeds were formulated on the basis of projecting the teaching of Scripture in a short and distilled form. Quite consciously, therefore, the church sought to summarize the scriptural message in its creeds, using scriptural terminology. The earliest opposition to the Nicene Creed was based on its inclusion of non-scriptural language, namely, using the term *homoousios* (same substance) to describe the relationship of the Father and the Son. The word *substance* could be located in Scripture, but one had to pluck the word out of its literary context to claim scriptural sanction for its use. But "same substance," also one word in Greek, was nowhere to be found. It was not until twenty-five years later that Athanasius would admit the fact, with the *proviso* that the

6. Though it is not found as a separately existing text, the Jerusalem creed was culled and reconstructed from Cyril's catechetical lectures. See J. N. D. Kelly, *Early Christian Creeds*, 3rd ed. (London: Longman, 1972), 183–84. Both the Jerusalem creed and the Caesarean creed predate the Nicene Creed, perhaps going back to the third century.

7. Rufinus, *Commentary on the Apostles' Creed* 2.

biblical message nevertheless proclaims the same teaching even if it does not use the exact terms.[8]

Florovsky insists that the doctrine of the creeds has a perennial adequacy because the church summarized the scriptural message in its major creeds. Whatever else may be said of the ancient creeds, it cannot be denied that they were deliberately constructed to be the epitome of the biblical message. If contemporary Christians find the creeds to be stumbling blocks because they seem opaque and difficult to understand, it may be that the same Christians find Scripture difficult to understand. "Let us remember that the early creeds were deliberately scriptural, however, and it is precisely their scriptural phraseology that makes them difficult for the modern man."[9]

Religious Instruction or Catecheses

The writing of what we call "theology" (the ancients did not use that term) was undertaken for many reasons, most of which had to do with understanding the Bible and clarifying how the Bible should be understood in light of the church's professed faith. It is a mistake to regard theology at this time as a metaphysical exercise detached from the intellectual, spiritual, and liturgical needs of congregations. Theology was an organic phenomenon; it grew and developed out of the communities that heard Scripture and professed the faith. Through this process, the seed of the church's early faith bloomed into various expressions: creeds, doctrines, hymns, and so on. These shared the basic affirmation of the credo "I believe" and sought to articulate an understanding of that profession. Augustine explains the dynamic inherent to the process in *On Catechising the Uninstructed*.

> The narration is full when each person is catechised in the first instance from what is written in the text, "In the beginning God created the heaven and the earth," on to the present times of the Church. This does not imply, however, either that we ought to repeat by memory the entire Pentateuch, and the entire Books of Judges, and Kings, and Esdras, and the entire Gospel and Acts of

---

8. In his work *De Decretum Nicaenum* (*On the Nicene Creed*).
9. Florovsky, *Bible, Church, Tradition*, 11.

the Apostles, if we have learned all these word for word; or that we should put all the matters which are contained in these volumes into our own words, and in that manner unfold and expound them as a whole. For neither does the time admit of that, nor does any necessity demand it. . . . But what we ought to do is, to give a comprehensive statement of all things, summarily and generally, so that certain of the more wonderful facts may be selected which are listened to with superior gratification, and which have been ranked so remarkably among the exact turning-points of the history.[10]

Typically, the most common context for providing an explanation of the basic message of Scripture and the creed was catechesis or oral instruction for candidates preparing for baptism.[11] Augustine offers a general review of the fundamental elements of the Christian faith in *On Catechizing* and the *Enchiridion* (below). Gregory of Nyssa does much the same thing in his *Address on Catechetical Instruction*. Without ever mentioning the creed, Gregory presents a theological narrative of salvation history supported by scriptural references and allusions, defending a pro-Nicene/Constantinopolitan position of the Trinity. He calls this narrative the "gospel revelation," and its overall end is to show both that Christ "is united to us in so far as he sustains existing things" and that "he united himself with our nature in order that by its union with the Divine, it might become divine."[12]

The works just mentioned were written to assist teachers involved in the task of church instruction. A number of sermons and addresses to catechumens (those receiving instruction) from the later fourth and fifth centuries also survive that are reflective of the catechizing process. This literature demonstrates that the process was becoming more formalized and unified as the church grew and received an ever larger number of converts. A female pilgrim to Jerusalem named Egeria alludes to the preparatory steps catechumens had to undergo during the forty-day period before Easter.[13] She observes that instruction on the creed as well as on doctrinal and moral issues was imparted to new believers.

10. Augustine, *On Catechising the Uninstructed* III.5.
11. "To catechize" in Greek means to instruct by word of mouth. A catechumen is one who is receiving instruction from a teacher.
12. Gregory of Nyssa, *Address on Catechetical Instruction* 25.
13. One English version is *Egeria: Diary of a Pilgrimage*, trans. G. E. Gingras (New York: Newman Press, 1970).

The actual course of instruction is found in a well-known set of addresses delivered by Cyril of Jerusalem to baptismal candidates during Lent of A.D. c. 350. Here he presents to catechumens the basics of the Christian faith through an exposition of the local church (Jerusalem) creed.[14]

At the outset, Cyril urges his listeners to persevere with the intensive classes of instruction because the goal is to arm them against error and provide a solid foundation for the Christian life. Herein was the path of discipleship. Cyril proceeds to lay forth ten points of instruction on God; Christ's divinity, incarnation, and passion; the Holy Spirit; the soul and the body; bodily resurrection; the centrality of Scripture; and the catholic church, all of which Cyril calls "indispensable teachings." Besides attending the sessions of instruction, the catechumens were required to renew their repentance, show the purity of their intention, and take seriously their preparation for baptism.

Preparing candidates for baptism also involved equipping them to receive the *traditio symboli*—the handing over of the creed. Integral to the catechumenate process was confiding the local church's creed to memory and understanding. The words of the church's creed contained, as Augustine told a group of new converts, "the words in which the faith of the mother Church is solidly based on the firm foundation which is Christ the Lord."[15] As the final stage of preparation before baptism on Easter, the *traditio* took place in many churches the Sunday before Easter. This is how it was done in Milan during the time of Bishop Ambrose, who described the creed as a "spiritual seal, which is our heart's meditation and, as it were, an ever present guard." In the *Explanation of the Creed*, Ambrose expounded on each clause of the Milanese creed, dividing it into twelve parts because it supposedly had derived from the faith of the twelve apostles.[16] Augustine, who was catechized and baptized by Ambrose, does not mention the apostolic legacy of the

14. These sequential addresses, or what Cyril called homilies, were transcribed from his oral presentations in one particular year. Most scholars think it was 350. For a full translation of the addresses, see W. Telfer, *Cyril of Jerusalem and Nemesius of Emesa* (Philadelphia: Westminster, 1955).

15. Augustine, *Sermon* 215.1.

16. Ambrose, *Explanation of the Creed* 10–11. Ambrose's assertion is based on the view that the Milanese creed was based on the Roman creed. Rufinus of Aquileia makes the same claim for the creed of Aquileia, also a derivative of the older Roman creed. It was from the Roman creed that the Apostles' Creed emerged.

creed but is no less firm in that it was necessary for a believer's complete conversion: "The creed builds you up in what you ought to believe and confess in order to be saved."[17]

The culmination of the delivery of the church's faith was the *redditio symboli:* a believer publicly giving back (reciting by memory) the creed before the congregation. Augustine calls the act of personally professing the church's creed a "holy martyrdom," "a holy witness to the truth of God."[18] What had been received from God was offered back to God as a symbol of a believer's commitment. This *redditio* too was an act of worship. It was a Christian's response to God, affirming what God had given, known through the tradition, and how it brought about the believer's transformation. It was at this moment, perhaps, when the vitality and power of the tradition was the closest to a believer.

Evangelicals can learn much from the ancient church's focus on catechesis, that is, on carefully instructing converts or those preparing to join the church in the biblical and doctrinal fundamentals of the Christian faith. In the preface to his manual of Christian instruction, Gregory of Nyssa declared:

> Religious catechism is an essential duty of the leaders "of the mystery of our religion" (1 Tim. 3:16). By it the Church is enlarged through the addition of those who are saved, while "the sure word which accords with the teaching" (Titus 1:9) comes within the hearing of unbelievers.[19]

We are in accord with Gregory's remarks when we insist that the teaching of new Christians or new members must go well beyond cursory explanations about the church's leadership, the congregational structure, and issues of stewardship as well as getting acquainted with the church's mission statement or a denominational summary. Too often we assume potential church members already know the fundamentals of the faith, whereas in reality they are often incapable of explaining even the basics of "the pattern of sound teaching" (2 Tim. 1:13). This need for equipping cannot be displaced in favor of simply giving one's own testimony anymore than a personal experience of the faith can be

17. Augustine, *Sermon* 214.1.
18. Augustine, *Sermon* 215.1.
19. Gregory of Nyssa, *Address on Catechetical Instruction* preface.

substituted for a reasonable grasp of that faith. If the church, as the apostle phrased it, is "the pillar and foundation of the truth" (1 Tim. 3:15), then the church's leadership must not shirk from the critical and time-consuming job of imparting Christian truth or catechizing those who profess to be Christian.

The Canon or Rule of Faith

Since the topic of the rule of faith was already introduced in chapter 2, this chapter need not add a great deal more, except to elaborate on the place of the rule as a conveyer of the tradition. Those elements of what the church believed, a propositional summary of "mere Christianity," are discovered in the *regula fidei*, rule of faith. As the word *rule* implies, it functioned as the standard or canon for orthodoxy. To be more precise, the rule did not function as a standard for the faith only; it was a distillation of the tradition in the sense that it was deemed to be synonymous with the apostolic faith itself.[20] This is borne out by Tertullian's reference to the rule as the "law of faith" or by the fact that he defined an apostate as one who had "lapsed from the Rule of faith."[21]

The dozen or so citations of the rule reveal that it was an elastic summary of the fundamental doctrines of Christianity. Analogous to the four accounts of the Gospels, the arrangement of the rule's content varied somewhat from one version to another without compromising its basic structure and unity. In fact, it seems that the rule was never fixed in a single or master version but was malleable to whatever didactic or polemical circumstances were at hand.

The first time we hear the phrase "canon of faith" is from Irenaeus of Lyons, who also calls it "the preaching," "the faith," or "the tradition." In the opening of his *Proof of the Apostolic Preaching*, he claims that Christians must adhere strictly to the "canon of faith" because it was handed down to them by the apostles and their disciples and because "it admonishes us to remember that we have received baptism for the remission of sins."[22] It is probable that the rule of faith

---

20. B. Hägglund, "Die Bedeutung der 'regula fidei' als Grundlage theologischer Aussagen," *Studia Theologia* 12 (1958): 23.

21. Tertullian, *On the Prescription of Heretics* 3.

22. Irenaeus, *Proof of the Apostolic Preaching* 3.

had its origination in the instruction designed for catechumens. But whatever its beginning, the rule functioned as an oral formulation of a common faith and pattern of teaching that came to serve a double duty of defending the faith against heresy. Irenaeus declared that the truth is found in the tradition of the apostles manifested to the world through the agency of the churches. In one passage, this tradition as the rule of faith is spelled out:

> The Church, though dispersed throughout the whole world, even to the ends of the earth, has received from the apostles and their disciples this faith: [she believes] in one God, the Father Almighty, Maker of heaven and earth, and the sea, and all things that are in them; and in one Christ Jesus, the Son of God, who became incarnate for our salvation; and in the Holy Spirit, who proclaimed through the prophets the dispensations of God, and the advents, and the birth from a virgin, and the passion, and the resurrection from the dead, and the ascension into heaven . . . and his [future] manifestation from heaven in the glory of the Father.[23]

In the works of a later contemporary, Tertullian from Carthage, the rule is cited on at least three separate occasions,[24] varying in length and details, which demonstrates that each citation is being accommodated to three distinct situations. The passage from *On the Prescription of Heretics* is the most comprehensive reference made to the rule:

> You must know that which prescribes the belief that there is only one God, and that He is none other than the Creator of the world, who produced all things out of nothing through His own Word, first of all things sent forth; that this Word is called His Son, and under the name of God, was seen variously by the patriarchs, heard always in the prophets, at last brought down by the Spirit and Power of the Father into the Virgin Mary, was made flesh in her womb, and, being born of her, went forth as Jesus Christ; thenceforth He preached the new law and the new promise of the kingdom of heaven, worked miracles; having been crucified, He

---

23. Irenaeus, *Against Heresies* 1.10.

24. Tertullian, *On the Prescription of Heretics* 13; idem, *On the Veiling of Virgins* 1; and idem, *Against Praxeas* 2. Smaller, more particularized segments of the rule Tertullian also mentions in passing, such as *On Prescription* 37; *Against Praxeas* 30; and *Against Marcion* IV.5.

rose again on the third day; having ascended into heaven, He sat at the right hand of the Father; sent the vicarious power of the Holy Spirit who leads the faithful; will come with glory to take the saints to the enjoyment of everlasting life and the celestial promises, and to condemn the wicked to everlasting fire, after a resurrection of both classes has been effected, together with the restoration of the flesh.[25]

Other citations of the rule can be found in the writings of Hippolytus, Origen, Cyprian, Novatian, Dionysius of Alexandria, and the *Didascalia apostolorum*, which all show basic structural similarities despite the external differences of language, location, and time. Certainly, the canon or rule of faith was not as static or as fixed as the early apologists might have us believe. There was no one rule of faith but rules, and when placed together they show a fluidity of wording and style. The basic structure of each varies between binitarian (Father and Son) and triadic (Father, Son, and Spirit). On each occasion that the rule was cited, it was obviously adapted to fit the writer's purpose and situation. Still, its various manifestations contain evidence of the shared essentials of the church's tradition, revealing a fairly cohesive platform of doctrinal norms to which one could appeal.

In the late fourth and early fifth centuries, there is occasional mention of the rule, though it appears that the notion of the rule had become more broadly construed than in earlier centuries. Sometimes it is used to represent a summary of the church's faith by indicating a set of confessional points, and sometimes it signifies a hermeneutical principle for rightly interpreting Scripture. Either way, the rule has a canonical character for ascertaining the heart of the biblical message, in terms of summarizing the Christian faith or by showing the proper means for determining the Christian faith. In Augustine's *On Christian Teaching*, for example, the latter use is usually at work. The rule, like a set of principles, enables a reader to read Scripture according to a christological interpretation in accordance with Nicene theology. Although the actual phrase "rule of faith" is not used, *On Christian Doctrine* I.5.5–19.21 provides readers with a credal-like recital of topics central to the faith, beginning with God and moving through the incarnation and the church to

25. Tertullian, *On the Prescription of Heretics* 13.

the bodily resurrection. Later in book III, Augustine says that the rule of faith is "perceived in the plainer passages of Scripture and in the authority of the church" and that he had already indicated the content of the rule in book I. It seems obvious that Augustine is referring to his earlier summarization of the faith. This is not the last time Augustine presents the church's rule in this narratival way.[26] In Augustine's manual of doctrinal instruction, the *Enchiridion*, the rule is invoked as a reference for the basics of the faith, closely identified with and even synonymously used for the church's creed.[27]

> What is the certain and distinctive foundation of the catholic faith? You would have the answers to all these questions if you really understood what one should believe, what one should hope for, and what one ought to love.[28]

The rule, then, guides an inquirer toward the content of the church's faith, hope, and love via the essentials of Christian belief: God as the Creator and goodness of all creation, the fall of humanity into sin, Jesus Christ the incarnate mediator, the role of the Holy Spirit in the Trinity, baptism and regeneration, the church, forgiveness of sins, the reality of the resurrection, and the life in the world to come. All this Augustine calls "our confession of faith," which is milk for spiritual infants but food for strong believers when it is pondered and studied.[29]

Bible Commentaries

Never before in history have so many critical editions of patristic commentaries and sermons, many of them translated into

26. See Augustine, *Against Faustus,* especially books 8 and 11; and idem, *Tractate* 98 on the Gospel of John. Earlier Latin writers seem to have done the same (Phoebadius of Agen, *Against the Arians* 22; and Eusebius of Vercelli, *On the Trinity* III.22, IV.19, VI.4).

27. Sometimes Augustine uses the term *faith* or *creed* for the rule of faith (*Enchiridion* XXX.114; and *Sermon* 398.1), though Lewis Ayres has argued that Augustine knows the two are not coterminus. He is equating the two because the creed summarizes the rule. See Lewis Ayres, "Augustine on the Rule of Faith: Rhetoric, Christology, and the Foundation of Christian Thinking," *Augustinian Studies* (forthcoming). A distinction between the creed as the doctrinal symbol of baptism and the rule as a didactic tool for explaining the creed had been historically long-standing.

28. Augustine, *Enchiridion* I.4.

29. Ibid., XXX.114.

English, been available as they are today. These commentaries were important as vehicles for transmitting the tradition. Unfortunately, written expositions on Scripture and homilies (originally oral expositions on Scripture) were often not distinguished from one another in late antique and medieval collections of an author's works. A given text or texts would be snatched from any part of a patristic author's writings based on thematic need (e.g., supplying a precedent for a discussion about observing a church law [canon law] on ordination or how to understand a passage from the Bible). It did not matter whether the text chosen was culled from a theological refutation, a homily, or a commentary as long as a patristic warrant for a contemporary practice could be found. Not until the fifteenth century did the writings of select fathers begin to be compiled and edited,[30] which also entailed making distinctions among the different kinds of literary genres present in an author's corpus. Our modern editions of patristic texts stand in debt to these earlier efforts.

Besides works of doctrinal theology, the age of the fathers was best known throughout the Middle Ages and the Reformation for its scriptural *expositiones*, or explanations of the meaning of biblical texts. We may call these "commentaries" as long as we understand that there was no generally accepted system of writing comments on biblical books, either in content or in form. Bear in mind that the division of the Old and New Testaments into chapters and verses was still a millennium away. There was no consensus about the format of analyzing biblical passages (i.e., whether sentence by sentence, paragraph by paragraph, or a mixture of both). Ancient writers used two approaches: (1) *scholia*, or detailed notes on a passage, and (2) commentary, which was a running explanation. Furthermore, there was no agreed-upon method for interpreting biblical passages, whether using a single approach (allegorical, historical, etc.) or a combination of approaches, which was usually the case.

The writing of running commentaries and analyses on the text of Scripture are not found in the ancient church until the late third century. Indeed, one cannot properly speak of exegesis until

---

30. Irena Backus, "The Early Church in the Renaissance and Reformation," in *Early Christianity: Origins and Evolution to A.D. 600*, ed. I. Hazlett, 291–303 (Nashville: Abingdon, 1991).

this time. Prior to the third century, the Bible had been used primarily as proof texts in controversies or as apology.[31] No practice of exegesis existed other than discovering how the Bible offered evidence or the norm for vindicating a theological point. Nevertheless, there was an abiding interest in and practice of the exposition of Scripture, as the New Testament itself bears witness. Besides Jesus' own frequent comments on Scripture, there are the examples of Peter expounding on the meaning of Joel 2:28–32 and several verses from Psalms (Pss. 16:8–11; 110:1). Philip the Evangelist was called on by the curious Ethiopian eunuch to render an interpretation of Isaiah 53 (Acts 8:26–35), and 2 Peter 3:15–16 contains a brief allusion to the exegesis of Paul's Epistles.

Fragments from an early second-century text in five books by Papias of Hierapolis, now lost, titled *Exegesis of the Lord's Sayings*, represent a kind of prototype in the interpretation of Christ's words and deeds in an ordered format.[32] The earliest scriptural expositions that survive, however, are the writings of Hippolytus in the West (writing in Greek) and Origen in the East. Hippolytus, associated with the church of Rome around A.D. 230, is said to have produced several expositions on certain Old Testament books and on Revelation.[33] Over two hundred books (a "book" corresponds to what a long chapter is today) are attributed to the encyclopedic efforts of Origen, who wrote *scholia* and commentaries on nearly the entire Old Testament (and on a good deal of the New). But these exercises of biblical exegesis were still rare when compared to the overall literary output of the time.

During the first decade of the fourth century, Victorinus of Poetovio produced commentaries on Genesis, Exodus, Leviticus, Isaiah, Ezekiel, Habakkuk, Ecclesiastes, Song of Solomon, Matthew, and Revelation.[34] He is the first Latin writer to be accredited with commentaries and whose example was followed within forty

31. J. H. Waszinck, "Tertullian's Principles and Methods of Exegesis," in *Early Christian Literature and the Classical Tradition: Mélanges R. M. Grant,* ed. W. Schoedel and R. Wilken, 9–31 (Paris: Beauchesne, 1979).

32. Eusebius of Caesarea, *Ecclesiastical History* III.39.1.

33. Of the Old Testament books, Genesis, Exodus, Isaiah, Daniel, Zechariah, Song of Solomon, Proverbs, and Ecclesiastes are named. Commentaries on select scriptural themes are also associated with this writer: *On the Six Days of Creation, On Saul, On the Antichrist, On the Passover,* and *On the Resurrection* (Jerome, *On Illustrious Men* 61).

34. Jerome, *On Illustrious Men* 74. Jerome mentions the commentary on Matthew elsewhere.

years by two Latin bishops, Hilary of Poitiers and Fortunatianus of Aquileia.[35] Roughly contemporary to Victorinus were exegetical works on Genesis and Song of Solomon by Methodius of Olympus.[36] Not until the middle to late fourth century, however, did commentary writing become a staple feature of conveying doctrine. A major reason for this development was the consistent practice of *sacra lectio* (reading of Scripture) in church services. Resembling the methods used in ancient Jewish synagogues, this practice was the liturgical use of scriptural texts. A biblical book or a series of books was read through consecutively from Sunday to Sunday (*lectio continua*). The sermon followed, resulting in a series of expositions on a given book.[37] By this means, a congregation heard most of the Bible read over time and also benefited from connected expositions of the text, enabling them to grasp sequences of events and the logic of arguments.

Readers of English have the benefit of accessing excerpted portions of patristic commentaries (and sermons) via three new series: The Church's Bible, The Ancient Christian Scripture Commentary, and The Navarre Bible. While it is arguable that excerpts of texts cannot offer the full meaning and impact of the primary sources, they nevertheless provide readers who have little or no acquaintance with patristic literature a wealth of texts already matched with relevant biblical passages. Each project has its own particular characteristics, and as a result, there is less overlap between the treatment of passages than one may think.[38] A shared goal for these volumes is the broadening and revitalization of scriptural study for teaching and preaching based on ancient

35. From Fortunatianus comes a commentary on the Gospels, now in fragmented condition, and Hilary's commentary on Matthew. Jerome tells of a commentary on the Song of Songs by Reticius of Autun (c. 314), but it does not survive.

36. Jerome, *On Illustrious Men* 83

37. For example, Augustine begins a sermon (*Sermon* 83) on Matthew 18:21–22 with the words, "Yesterday, the holy gospel . . . [cites 18:15–17]. Today the passage that follows this, which we heard when it was read just now, deals with the same point."

38. The Church's Bible and The Ancient Christian Scripture Commentary are arranged according to the *cantena* style, linking a number of brief patristic comments together on a given passage of Scripture. The same can be said of The Navarre Bible (though with shorter segments), but it provides texts from the whole range of Roman Catholic authorities: "documents of the Magisterium, exegesis by Fathers and Doctors of the Church, works by important spiritual writers (usually saints, of every period), and writings of the founder of our University" (8). Included also is Vulgate Latin for each passage and various grammatical and textual observations.

resources. At the very least, these series demonstrate that the Christian church has a long tradition of commentary on the Bible, far older (and richer) than the scholarship of the late nineteenth and twentieth centuries on which nearly all present methods and studies are based. This is a matter that Bible schools, lay institutes, seminaries, and faculties of theology should pay heed in their training of students in biblical interpretation. The historical-critical methods of the nineteenth and twentieth centuries that have dominated the scholarly approach used in institutions of higher education are surprisingly uncritical of themselves and have significantly narrowed the playing field of interpretation. Patristic and medieval forms of "pre-critical" exegesis—scriptural and theological—need to be retrieved as having important value for biblical interpretation and application.

Homilies

The other most common source of biblical commentary was the sermon or homily. Since the vast majority of patristic theologians were bishops or other clergy, it stands to reason that their efforts were devoted mainly to the preparation and delivery of sermons. Preaching occurred on Saturdays and Sundays and even daily during Lent and the week after Easter. In the case of Augustine, it is estimated that he preached between eight and ten thousand sermons, many of these being recorded at the time by stenographers (known as *notarii*). Over a thousand of his sermons survive.[39]

Collections of sermons, once put into written form and edited, often functioned as a running commentary on a biblical book or a large portion of it. Chrysostom's homilies on Matthew are a good case in point. The bishop began his series by introducing the Gospel:

> Filled with the Spirit, Matthew wrote what he wrote—Matthew the tax collector. I am not ashamed to call him by his profession,

39. Augustine's sermons are now readily available in English in *The Works of St. Augustine: A Translation for the Twenty-first Century*, part 3, vols. 1–11, trans. Edmund Hill (Hyde Park, N.Y.: New City Press, 1990–98).

neither him nor the others; after all, this it is in particular that brings out the Spirit's grace and these men's virtue. He was within his rights to refer to his work as Gospel, Good News: it was, in fact, abolition of punishment, forgiveness of sins, righteousness, holiness, redemption, sonship, inheriting heaven, and kinship with the Son of God that Jesus went about announcing to every-one—to hostile people, to ungrateful people, to people sitting in darkness. So what could ever match these good tidings? God on earth, man in heaven.[40]

Chrysostom preached ninety sermons on the Gospel while he was in Antioch (c. 390). They were later edited and published as a whole, representing the oldest complete commentary on the first Gospel. Augustine's works *Tractates on the Gospel of John* and *Tractates on the Epistle of 1 John* were composed of 124 and ten sermons respectively. But of course not all patristic sermons were exegetical in the strict sense of sustained comments on a given biblical text. It is obvious that sermons 81–94 of Caesarius of Arles were structured around a study of the leading personali-ties of Genesis.[41] Many of Leo of Rome's sermons, as was quite common, dealt with the special days of the church calendar year: Easter, Christmas, epiphany, Lent, ascension, and Pentecost. Many homilies were also topical or thematic. A sampling of col-lections and individual sermons[42] shows that all facets of Chris-tian life and liturgical practice, feast days, martyrdom, doctrine, and social issues were addressed in congregations.

The great mistake is to assume that sermons were not as sig-nificant as doctrinal and polemical treatises for transmitting serious Christian thought. Too often scholars have looked to major theological works to ascertain the substance of an ancient thinker's views. Sermons, on the other hand, have been regarded as largely incidental to doctrinal construction because they are popular forms of communication. But such a dichotomy mis-construes the patristic evidence according to biases of how the

---

40. Chrysostom, *Homily* 1. More than nine hundred sermons of Chrysostom are extant, though this represents only five and a half years out of a total of twelve years of preaching. See W. Mayer and P. Allen, *John Chrysostom* (London: Routledge, 2000), 7.

41. E.g., "On the Call of the Blessed Abraham," "On Jacob's Ladder," "On the Blessed Joseph."

42. See n. 38.

academic and the popular were in tension with each other.[43] We create divisions between the practical and the technical, assuming that the early church did likewise. In fact, ancient preachers considered the sermon to be an appropriate venue for both pastoral exhortation and doctrinal instruction. Surely a difference existed between the educated and the uneducated, between the literate and the illiterate in the ancient world. Yet it is no less the case that bishops considered the homily to be a serious forum for intellectual inquiry. The sermon was not for providing theology in a dumbed-down version, simplifying ideas to the point of losing nuances and implications. Sermons dealt with substantial moral issues related to the Christian life, and they also communicated critical concepts, presenting both the basic tenets of the faith as well as more complicated doctrinal points.[44] For all those who would investigate the thought and life of the fathers, their sermons are indispensable.

Theological Hymnody

Just before Easter in A.D. 386, Ambrose, the bishop of Milan, found himself and his congregation besieged by imperial soldiers. The emperor Valentinian II, who sponsored an "Arian" form of faith,[45] demanded that the bishop hand over one of the basilicas in the city. Ambrose refused. Tensions rose throughout the city, and the threat of riot became real. During Holy Week, armed men were sent to take by force the church where Ambrose was presiding. While soldiers surrounded the building, packed with the faithful, Ambrose decided to teach the congregation hymns. Augustine was an eyewitness of the event, being a catechumen at the time, and he tells us that the church at Milan had only recently begun the custom of singing together for mutual comfort and exhortation.

43. Stanley P. Rosenberg, "Interpreting Atonement in Augustine's Preaching," in *The Glory of the Atonement*, ed. C. E. Hill and F. A. James III, 221–38 (Downers Grove, Ill.: InterVarsity, 2004).

44. Ibid., 11.

45. To be exact, a "Homoian" form of faith: the Son is like (*homoios*) the Father who begat him.

The impact these hymns had on the minds of the congregants was made clear by Ambrose himself, who reported in a sermon that "Arian" detractors had accused him of leading the people astray by his hymns. He writes, "I certainly do not deny it. That is a lofty strain and there is nothing more powerful than it. For what has more power than the confession of the Trinity. . . . All eagerly vie with another in confessing the faith, and know how to praise in verse the Father, the Son and the Holy Spirit."[46]

These Milanese hymns and chants provided believers with more than inspiration and pious sound bites about their faith. Ambrose's intent was to reinforce key features of Nicene theology. But as dramatic as these circumstances were, the creative inculcation of Christian truths through recitation and song was not an unfamiliar practice. Since the days of the apostles, the worship of the church served as a critical vehicle for imparting *doctrina*, that is, ordered teaching about the Christian faith. Christian leaders of the early centuries found that worship was a good opportunity to supply believers with the concrete foundations of how to think and live Christianly. There was, in fact, a reciprocal relationship between worship and doctrine, between the act of praise and the task of theology. Like homilies, early hymns and theological poetry were constructive exercises in conveying the tradition. Surely it is no accident that a worshiper recalled the crisis in Milan years afterward with the words, "The sounds flowed into my ears and the truth was distilled into my heart."[47]

Of course, the canonical Psalms was the primary hymnbook of the church from the beginning. But soon Christian leaders orchestrated small hymnic or poetic lines as a means of imparting the framework of the tradition into the minds and hearts of believers. Given the likelihood of illiteracy among most Christians, learning the faith by recitation in rhyme was essential. One of the earliest known instances of this method is found in what Paul called "the mystery of godliness":

> He appeared in a body,
>   was vindicated by the Spirit,

46. Ambrose, *Against Auxentius* 34.
47. Augustine, *Confessions* IX.6.14.

> was seen by angels,
>> was preached among the nations,
> was believed on in the world,
>> was taken up in glory.

1 Timothy 3:16[48]

The content of this poem is densely packed and imparts crucial truths about the equal realities of Christ's physical appearance in the world and his heavenly origin and purpose. In just a few lines, the faithful confess the universal nature of Christ's person while avoiding the extreme of exalting Jesus' divinity at the expense of his humanity, not an uncommon problem by the middle of the first century. Other examples of hymnody can be found in the epistles of the New Testament.[49]

An anonymous work from the early second century called *2 Clement* is arguably one of the earliest extrabiblical examples of a Christian sermon. It appears to draw on the material of the Synoptic Gospels as well as oral Jesus traditions independent of the written Gospels.[50] The first chapter also contains some verses (4–8), in part or whole, of a theological confession, rendered here poetically in order to emphasize the original source on which it seems to be drawing.

> He has given us the light;
> As a father, he has called us sons;
> He has saved us when we were perishing.

---

48. The poetic or hymnic origin of this passage becomes more evident when we observe that it is structured in three antithetical pairs, as construed above. In each pair, a *datum* from the Jesus tradition is presented within a contrast setting of the heavenly/spiritual and earthly/material. The focus is clearly on the process by which God revealed himself in Christ.
    1. related to the incarnation—God has come in the flesh/confirmed by the Spirit
    2. related to the gospel proclaimed—testified by angels (at birth or resurrection)/ preached among nations
    3. related to the consequences of his coming—believed in the world/ascends to heaven.

49. E.g., Phil. 2:5–11; 2 Tim. 2:11–13.

50. Karl Paul Donfried, *The Setting of Second Clement in Early Christianity* (Leiden: Brill, 1974), 56. Use of the term *graphē* in *2 Clement* 2.4 insinuates that the writer had access to some collection of the Lord's sayings, but it is not clear whether the written Gospels as we know them are being placed on a par with the Old Testament.

What praise shall we give him? What payment in return for
  what we have received?

Our minds were blinded;
We worshiped stones, and wood, and gold, and silver and
  brass—works of men.
Our whole life was nothing else but death.
We were thus wrapped in darkness and our vision filled with
  thick mist.
We recovered our sight by His will, laying aside the cloud which
  enveloped us.

He had mercy upon us, and in His compassion,
He saved us when we had no hope of salvation, except what
  comes from Him, though He had seen in us much
  deception and destruction.

He called us when we did not exist, and out of nothing,
He willed us into being.

In a style reminiscent of the Psalms, these lines celebrate the
sovereign purposes of God through the redemption of his people,
who are undeserving.

As shown above, in the fourth century, the practice of using hymns
to convey sound doctrine became widespread. A famous orator in the
city of Rome, Marius Victorinus, converted late in life to Christianity, an event described by Augustine in his *Confessions.* Sometime
after his baptism, Victorinus wrote several technical philosophical
works defending the Nicene form of faith, which contemporaries
said could be understood only by the very learned.[51] About the same
time, he composed a set of three hymns. Victorinus was the first Latin
intellectual to make a defense of the Nicene faith, and his hymns
provided another avenue for his efforts. It may be that his hymns,
on account of their simpler terms, did greater good than his treatises
in extending sound trinitarian teaching in the church.

The *First Hymn* opens with the words:

True Light, assist us,
  O God the Father all powerful!

51. Jerome, *On Illustrious Men* 101.

> Light of Light, assist us,
>   mystery and power of God!
> Holy Spirit, assist us,
>   the bond between Father and Son!
> In repose you are Father,
>   in your procession, the Son,
> And binding all in One, you are the Holy Spirit.[52]

Reference made to "Light of Light" is a clear allusion to the Son, who is described in the Nicene Creed as "God from God, Light from Light, True God from True God." In keeping with the pro-Nicene trinitarian agenda, the hymn comes to the conclusion:

> Christ is therefore all, hence Christ is mystery.[53]
> Through him, all things, in him, all things, for him, all things!
> He himself is the whole whose depth is the Father,
> By his procession, he is length and width of the Father.
> Hence Christ appearing in time to teach the depth and, indeed,
>   the mystery.[54]
> And Christ hiding within, teaching interiorly, is the Holy Spirit.[55]

Three hymns are also attributed to Hilary of Poitiers, writing less than a decade after Victorinus, but only one is securely attested. This one comes from the hymnal of the ancient Irish church (Codex Aretinus) and is titled "An Ode to Christ the King."

> Let the faithful sing a hymn,
> Let our song echo forth,
>   To Christ the King we render our debt of praises.
>
> You are the Word
> from the heart of God,
>   You are the Way, You are the Truth.

---

52. Marius Victorinus, *First Hymn*, in *Marius Victorinus: Theological Treatises on the Trinity,* trans. Mary T. Clark (Washington, D.C.: Catholic University of America Press, 1981), 315.
53. Cf. Eph. 3:9.
54. Eph. 3:10.
55. Victorinus, *First Hymn*, 319.

You are called the root of Jesse, You are, we read, the Lion.
You are the Father's right hand, the Mount, the Lamb, the
    Cornerstone, the Bridegroom,
God, the Dove, Fire, Shepherd, and the Door.

You, who were born into our world, are found in the prophets.
You, who were before all time, are the Maker of time's
    beginning.
    You are the creator of heaven, of earth, gathering the seas.

You make the lame to walk, the blind to see the light.
You cleansed the leper by a word
    and made alive the dead.

You commanded water to wine turn.
You fed five thousand with but five loaves, two fish,
    in twelve baskets leftovers provided.

Let the faithful celebrate His glory,
which will remain with us, singing and entreating, throughout
    eternity,
    together, let us celebrate the immensity of your majesty.

We sing to Christ the King, the Lord![56]

As mentioned above, Ambrose made a lasting impact on the doctrinal awareness of the Milanese congregation by teaching them hymns. The best-known hymn of the famous bishop is "God, Creator of All Things."

> God, Creator of all things
>   and Ruler of the heavens, fitting
> the day with beauteous light,
>   and night with the grace of sleep.
>
> Now the day is over and night begun,
>   we sing to you a hymn,
> With thanks and asking that you loose us
>   from our sinfulness.

56. A. S. Walpole, *Early Latin Hymns* (Cambridge: Cambridge University Press, 1922), 5–15.

From the depth of our hearts, we praise you,
  our ringing voices cry out to you,
With holy affection, we love you,
  our ready minds adore you.

So when the deep gloom of night
  closes in upon the day,
Let our faith not know darkness,
  and the night shine with hope.

As the depth of our heart casts aside unclean thoughts,
  let it dream of you,
nor let worry of the enemy's schemes,
  disturb us in peace.

We beseech Christ and the Father,
  and the Spirit of Christ and the Father,
One power over all,
  O Trinity, strengthen us we pray.[57]

Turning farther east to Syriac-speaking Christianity, Ephraem of Nisibis (the Syrian) wrote a number of nonprose works in the mid-fourth century, especially hymns on themes that mark the Christian life: faith, the church, fasting, and other biblical themes. Among those hymns that commemorate the major events of Christ's ministry are hymns on his birth, baptism, crucifixion, and resurrection. His best known are the hymns on the nativity. Not noted perhaps for their theological originality, these hymns seem to function rather as poetic moments of reflection on the mysteries of God's revelation of himself in the world. While scholars are uncertain about the hymns' intended audience, it seems likely that they were written for the congregation in Nisibis, Ephraem's church home.[58] For each of the hymns, a melody is stipulated at the beginning for the purpose of singing it. The melody is no longer known, but it must have been apparent to the church. Hymn 3 on the nativity is one of thanksgiving and praise, focusing on the paradoxical nature of almighty God becoming a helpless infant.

57. Ibid., 46–49.
58. Due to the occupation of Nisibis by the Persians, Ephraem relocated to the city of Edessa in 363 for the last ten years of his life.

(To the melody, "He consoled with promises")
Blessed be the Child Who today delights Bethlehem.
Blessed be the Newborn Who today made humanity young
    again.
Blessed be the Fruit Who bowed Himself down for our hunger.
Blessed be the Gracious One Who suddenly enriched
    all our poverty and filled our need.
Blessed be He Whose mercy inclined Him to heal our sickness.

    Refrain: My Lord, blessed be Your Child,
        Who raised to honor our hardness of heart.

Glory to that Hidden One Whose Child was revealed.
Glory to the Living One Whose Child became a mortal.
Glory to the Great One Whose Son descended and became
    small.
Glory to the One Power Who fashioned Him,
    The image of His greatness and form for His hiddenness.[59]

In his hymns written for the Feast of Epiphany, Ephraem celebrates the scriptural themes associated with that day: the Magi's appearance and Jesus' baptism by John. A few lines from the first (of fifteen) hymns read as follows:

In the Height and the Depth, the Son had two heralds: the star
    which proclaimed Him from above;
John who also preached Him from below. Two heralds, earthly
    and heavenly.

The herald from above showed His nature to be from the Most
    High,
And that He was from beneath showed his body to be from
    humankind.
Wondrous amazement that His divinity and His humanity by
    them were proclaimed!

Whosoever reckons Him of earth only, the star of light will con-
    vince him that He is of heaven;
Whosoever reckons Him of spirit only, John will convince him
    that He is also bodily.

59. *Ephraem the Syrian: Hymns*, ed. and trans. Kathleen McVey (Mahwah, N.J.: Paulist Press, 1989), 82–83.

The whole creation became for Him as one mouth and cried out
    concerning Him:
The Magi cry out with their gifts; the barren cry out with their
    children; the star of light
—lo, it cries out in the sky, "Behold the Son of the King"!

The heavens are opened, the waters break forth, the dove is in
    glory!
The voice of the Father is stronger than thunder as it utters the
    word, "This is My Beloved."
The angels brought tidings, the children acclaimed Him in their
    hosannas.[60]

Though we have considered only a few examples, the reader
of patristic literature will quickly discover that the most astute
thinkers of the age could effectively frame the faith in verse. Again,
these poetic works were just as effective as, if not more effective
than, polemical and theological treatises in teaching believers
Christian truth.

Major Works of Theology

It may be an overstatement to say that writing theological treatises was perceived as a devotional activity for the edification and
defense of the church, but not by much. The leading theological
productions of the early church are properly regarded as doctrinal treatises that were meant to clarify key points of Christian
thought. One thinks immediately of Irenaeus's *Against Heresies*,
Tertullian's *Against Marcion* and *Against Praxeas*, Cyprian's *On
the Unity of the Catholic Church*, Athanasius's *On the Incarnation
of the Word*, Ambrose of Milan's *On the Faith*, Gregory of Nyssa's
Against Eunomius, Basil of Caesarea's *On the Holy Spirit*, Gregory
of Nazianzus's *Theological Orations*, Augustine's *City of God*, Leo
of Rome's *Tome*, and Cyril of Alexandria's *Treasury of the Holy and
Consubstantial Trinity*—works that have acted as milestones in
the construction of the Christian doctrine of God and the divine
acts of creation and re-creation. At the same time, such works

60. Translation (slightly altered), in *The Nicene and Post-Nicene Fathers*, 2nd series,
vol. 13, ed. P. Schaff and H. Wace (Grand Rapids: Eerdmans, 1987), 266.

went hand in hand with prayer and a sense that the quest for truth about God called for a life that was being transformed by God. For example, Hilary of Poitiers ends his lengthy twelve-book examination of the relationship between Father and Son with a concluding prayer:

> Keep, I pray O Lord, this my pious faith undefiled, and even till my spirit departs, grant that this may be the utterance of my convictions. May I ever hold fast to that which I professed in the creed of my regeneration,[61] when I was baptized in the Father, and the Son and the Holy Spirit. Let me, in short, adore You, our Father, and Your Son together with You; let me find the mercy of your Holy Spirit, Who is from You, through the Only-Begotten. For I have a convincing witness to my faith, Who says, "Father, all mine is Yours and Yours is mine" (Jn. 17:10), even my Lord Jesus Christ, Who dwells in You, and is from You, and is with You, forever God: Who is blessed forever and ever. Amen.[62]

Augustine likewise concludes his last book of *On the Trinity* with a lengthy prayer as a fitting culmination of the whole.

> Directing my attention toward this rule of faith as best I could, as far as you enabled me to, I have sought you and desired to see intellectually what I have believed, and I have argued much and toiled much. O Lord my God, my one hope, listen to me lest out of weariness I should stop wanting to seek you, but let me seek your face always, and with ardor. Do you yourself give me the strength to seek, having caused yourself to be found and having given me the hope of finding you more and more. Before you lies my strength and my weakness; preserve the one, heal the other. Before you lies my knowledge and my ignorance; where you have opened to me, receive me as I come in; where you have shut to me, open to me as I knock. Let me remember you, let me understand you, let me love you. Increase these things in me until you refashion me entirely.
>
> O Lord the one God, God the Trinity, whatsoever I have said in these books is of you, may those that are yours acknowledge; whatsoever of myself alone, do you and yours forgive. Amen.[63]

61. A reference not to the Nicene Creed but to his baptismal faith.
62. Hilary Poitiers, *On the Trinity* XII.57.
63. Augustine, *On the Trinity* XV.51.

Augustine was so acutely aware that his inquiry into the trinitarian mystery was a devotional work that one translator has portrayed *On the Trinity* as a "quest for, or exploration of, the mystery of the Trinity as a complete program for the Christian spiritual life, a program of conversion, and renewal and discovery of self in God and God in self."[64] There can be no question that the work was no less polemical, as especially apparent in its earlier books. *On the Trinity* is manifestly anti-Arian (*homoion*) as well as anti-modalist and constructs a trinitarian theology that is conscious of refuting the claims of its opponents. Augustine understands that such refutation is necessary for the very reason that doctrine nourishes the church and so enables the clarification of its earthly and spiritual vision. Our conception and appropriation of God as Trinity, or what he called "contemplation," must be grounded on having the right mind about God. This is no mere task of intellection for the Christian thinker. Because the Son was inseparable from the Father, and the Spirit from the unity of the Father and the Son, all the works of Jesus and the Holy Spirit are the works of God. A Christian is thereby fulfilled in the happiness for which he or she was meant: "For the fullness of our happiness, beyond which there is none else, is this: to enjoy God the Three in whose image we were made."[65] Knowing that this is the goal, believers seek to clarify the vision of God by "enticing our sickly gaze"[66] toward "the things which are above and forsake the things which are below (Col. 3:1)."[67] As we do this by faith and in hope, our vision becomes clearer and our motives in living the Christian life become purer.

Indeed, the writing of theology was itself a sacred task and required pure hands. As far as Gregory of Nazianzus was concerned, the practice of theology is "to cleanse the theologian." In keeping with this understanding, he begins the first of his five theological *Orations* with an admonition that sets the tone for the whole:

> Discussion of theology is not for everyone, I tell you, not for everyone—it is no such inexpensive or effortless pursuit. . . . It is

---

64. *Saint Augustine: The Trinity,* trans. Edmund Hill (New York: New City Press, 1991), 19.

65. Augustine, *On the Trinity* I.3.18.

66. That is, our "inclination."

67. Augustine, *On the Trinity* I.1.2.

for those who have been tested and have a sound footing in study and, more importantly, have undergone, or at least are undergoing, purification of body and soul. For one who is not pure to lay hold of pure things is dangerous, just as it is for weak eyes to look at the sun's brightness.[68]

Gregory's concern was not that theology was an intellectual process but that it should not be reduced to an intellectual exercise, to a matter of proper dialectical method regardless of truth uttered. In seeking divine truth—undergoing its mental struggle and moral challenges—will we take the "next step . . . to look at ourselves and to smooth the theologian within us, like a statue, into beauty."[69] Theology was both to nurture and to educate, to foster *paideia*.[70] It was supposed to fulfill the biblical mandate of purifying the self. At the same time, this first book was a theological invective, that is, a rhetorical refutation "Against the Eunomians" to garner support against them. Yet Gregory was seeking the truth about the nature of theology such that the Eunomians were proved false. In the process, readers are brought into the benefits of sharing the theological task.

However we may qualify the literary style of major theological works (polemical, protreptic, etc.), they cannot be easily separated from the pastoral goals that absorbed nearly every patristic writer. Rather unlike the modern orientation, the theological task could not be separated from spirituality. Nor was spirituality an existential matter that regarded the cultivation of the mind as extraneous to its goals. Indeed, cultivating the eyesight of the mind, so to speak, had been a central component of the philosopher's goal, before and during the time of Christianity. Christian thinkers, no less, saw such a goal as incumbent upon the theological task. Definition, qualification, and elucidation were paths by which Christians could be directed to faith, hope, and love. In effect, theology was regarded as a work of holiness. This is the great legacy left to us by the early fathers.

68. Gregory of Nazianzus, *Oration* 27.3, in *Faith Gives Fullness to Reasoning: The Five Theological Orations of Gregory of Nazianzus*, ed. Frederick Norris, trans. L. Wickham and F. Williams (Leiden: Brill, 1991), 218.

69. Ibid., 27.7.

70. See Norris, introduction to ibid., 17–39. *Paideia* is the process by which learning about God transforms the self and leads to purification of body and soul.

Postscript

THIS BOOK WAS not an attempt to persuade evangelicals to embrace a particular ecclesiastical perspective. I myself am planted within the free church tradition and intend to stay there. Of course, some free church Christians end up taking a "high church" route, but that is not what I am advocating here. Instead, I have been arguing for a new reform of the old reforms that gave birth to the various families of faith known as Protestantism. My hope is that the energy of evangelical piety, with its emphasis on personal conversion, could be adapted to and shaped by the faith of the early church's tradition. It is a realistic goal. There are certain religious impulses that the free church and the early church share in common, as a recent set of articles on this subject has suggested.[1] The ideas proposed in that collection are but a beginning, and while the search for commonalities always risks artificiality, at the very least, characteristics of spirituality and biblical literacy exist that the two can gain from each other. After all, the patristic tradition is an indigenous part of the history of Protestant evangelicalism, whether conscious to many of its believers or not. As discussed earlier, some of the features of the apostolic and patristic church are part of the DNA, as it were, of the nature of evangelicalism.

1. D. H. Williams, ed., *The Free Church and the Early Church: Essays in Bridging the Historical and Theological Divide* (Grand Rapids: Eerdmans, 2002).

Evangelicals simply need to look beyond their own experience into the broader heritage of the Christian faith.

The problem is that too many of these features have been forgotten or ignored for the reasons reviewed earlier. Meanwhile, evangelicalism is becoming increasingly relativized by the social contexts, mainly Western, that it inhabits. While no Christian tradition can prevent itself from becoming partly enculturated, the question arises, How much should Christians accommodate their faith to culture in order to speak to that culture? How can one become all things to all people without becoming no longer oneself? As evangelicalism continues to lower its doctrinal and ethical "walls" in the name of providing a user-friendly church, what is it able to offer to those who discover Christian conversion, not merely through their own experiences of God but as participants in the historic faith and practice of the church? In short, what message is evangelicalism able to give society that culture is not already giving it?

Theological commentators have noted many times that evangelicalism is suffering from a loss of coherency, as the very content of the historic faith no longer informs the central task of the church. Preaching easily slips into the mode of moralizing or anecdotal storytelling, and eventually the flock of God can no longer stomach a diet that might cause them to think deeply about the content of the Christian faith.[2] Congregations are well schooled in neatly dividing the faith into practical and theoretical aspects, convinced that only the former are of concern to them. Theology is therefore an elective of the Christian life, not necessary and too divisive for a religion of civility. In their quest to reach culture, evangelical congregations have come to reflect the cultural preferences of their audiences: anti-institutional, informal, nondogmatic, therapeutic, and unaware of the difference between tolerance and moral confusion.

Yet many evangelicals are discovering that no amount of creative packaging and marketing of the gospel will rescue church ministry if they lose the theological center that enables them to define the

2. David Wells, *No Place for Truth, or Whatever Happened to Evangelical Theology?* (Grand Rapids: Eerdmans, 1993); idem, *Losing Our Virtue: Why the Church Must Recover Its Moral Vision* (Grand Rapids: Eerdmans, 1998); and E. T. Oakes, "Evangelical Theology in Crisis," *First Things* 36 (October 1993): 38–44.

faith and prescribe the kinds of intellectual and practical relations it should have in the world. Given the centrifugal and atomistic forces already inherent among free church and evangelical forms of Christianity, the lack of an identifying center is spiritually and intellectually debilitating. Over half a century ago, Henri de Lubac raised a question in his study of Catholicism that is still strikingly relevant: "Does not neglect of dogma increase the extent of moral failure?"[3] Separating the two (doctrine and morality) not only is a violation of the catholic spirit but also fails to understand the nature of the Christian life. Lest we forget, the Israelites' worship and approach to God were enshrined in the Ten Commandments, where thought and practice were symbiotic ways of honoring God as Creator and Lord. "You shall have no other gods before me" was a theological statement that implied some very practical issues.

Let me also restate that the proposal of a *ressourcement* of the early church's faith for evangelicals is not a betrayal of the evangelical spirit any more than it was for the catholic spirit when it was called forth as part of the Roman Catholic renewal in the mid-twentieth century. Evangelical *ressourcement* is rather the necessary next step for contemporary evangelicalism that it might grow with theological integrity and ecumenical prudence in a cultureless culture and Christless spirituality. If, indeed, the church must create its own culture to preserve a distinctive existence in the midst of the decay of Western culture,[4] then such resources are critical fonts for believers to discover their roots and Christian identity.

Part of the new reform of the old reforms is that the tradition of the early church should not be used as a polemical device by evangelical Protestants (or Roman Catholics or Eastern Orthodox) to disprove the historical and spiritual legitimacy of the others. The anti-Catholic polemics and revisionist histories that have marked Protestant apologetic literature for the last three centuries have not been successful either in discrediting the Roman Catholic Church or in unifying Protestants. The appeal to the Bible as the only infallible rule, stripped of its historical packaging of church

3. Henri de Lubac, *Catholicism: Christ and the Common Destiny of Man*, trans. L. C. Sheppard and E. Englund (San Francisco: Ignatius Press, 1988), 15.

4. As argued in Ralph Wood, *Contending for the Faith: The Church's Engagement with Culture* (Waco: Baylor University Press, 2003).

and tradition, has not established a more certain or harmonious interpretation. J. I. Packer is correct in declaring that the Reformation is over, by which he means that the forging of our Protestant identity should no longer be done in the furnace of heated anti-Catholicism. Protestantism's own identity is inescapably hinged to the Roman Catholic identity, as Karl Barth quipped after he attended part of Vatican II. Without continuously engaging Roman Catholicism both critically and constructively, the claim to catholicity from the side of the Reformation churches remains empty. This engagement is what Barth referred to as "dialectical catholicity," a course that he steered between the neo-Protestantism of his day and Roman Catholicism. Only if one occupies a "common room" that exists for both sides can the other continue, as Barth phrases it, to become a question to oneself. It is when we remain in an authentic tension of questioning ourselves that the benefits of the Reformation—"once reformed, always in the process of being reformed"—are served.[5]

Without doubt, the early tradition offers the most trustworthy way of future dialogue between the major dissenting Christian churches. As has been shown time and time again in the theological venues of the World Council of Churches and similar initiatives, the patristic age provides an avenue for an ecumenism faithful to Scripture and the church precisely because it is foundational to all church communions. The canons of faith and text erected in the patristic period provide a kind of doctrinal, liturgical, and practical hallway into which the "rooms" of Roman Catholicism, Eastern Orthodoxy, and Protestantism open. In this hallway, we may meet and discover some common ground—the bedrock—for all three major families that precedes any one claim upon it, which we may believe and defend together.

A marvelous and unexpected example of this dynamic can be found in the heart of Texas. The Development of Early Catholic Christianity Seminar (also called the Second Century Seminar) is a twice-a-semester meeting of professors, pastors, and priests from a number of academic institutions and religious affiliations that has convened several times since the early 1970s. Out of this group have come many of the contributions of Albert Outler, Wil-

---

5. Karl Barth, *Ad Limina Apostolorum: An Appraisal of Vatican II*, trans. K. R. Crim (Richmond: John Knox, 1968). In this essay, Barth coins the phrase "evangelical catholic."

liam Farmer, Denis Farkasfalvy, Everett Ferguson, and others in areas of church history, patristic studies, and Bible. What mutually exclusive denominational positions will not allow, this academic setting has provided and continues to provide for younger scholars with a heart for the church. Through shared texts and critical responses to the early fathers, this group has explored the bases of doctrines and practices that are common denominators for the Christian identity. Here ecumenism is seen at its best as this group has sought the place of historical and theological consensus in the light of fidelity to the biblical and traditional sources.

Other steps of the new reform involve discovering in this post-Reformation age that the Bible is most faithfully understood not merely by the tools of literary, historical, and form criticism but through the lenses of the church's canonical tradition. We need to regain the richness of scriptural interpretation and imagination by disallowing modern critical theory the sole prerogative in exegesis. Certainly, enormous strides have been made in the last century of biblical scholarship, but there have been losses as well.[6] To accept the authority of the tradition is to embrace the principle that biblical interpretation ultimately belongs in the church, not in the academy. The tradition also gives the church a foundation for preserving the essentials of the Christian message in its reading of the Bible. Augustine's oft-quoted remark comes to mind: "I should not have believed the gospel if the authority of the catholic church had not moved me."[7] Reflecting back to his pre-Christian days, Augustine remembers the simplicity of his mind and how various voices close to him, heretical and otherwise, were promoting their interpretations of the Bible as truth. The authority of the catholic church, however, was the means by which one heard the gospel. The gospel and the preaching of catholicity belonged together. Augustine had no intention of subordinating the gospel to the church; he simply wanted to emphasize that the gospel is always received in the context of the church's catholic preaching (i.e., the tradition). What better place to hear the exposition of biblical meaning than within the faith, nourished and structured according to the Bible?

6. David Steinmetz, "The Superiority of Pre-Critical Exegesis," *Theology Today* 37 (1980–81): 27–38.

7. Augustine, *Against the Fundamental Epistle of Mani* 6.

Finally, let me say that the patristic faces evangelicals will meet in the hallway of common ground will not all be familiar or comfortable. Clearly, the ancient Christians had ways of expressing themselves and their times that are unfamiliar to us today. Moreover, there are some foreign aspects of the patristic church to which evangelicals are unaccustomed (e.g., asceticism as a preferred way of spirituality, the powers of saints, or the allegorical use of Scripture). Contrary to the view that the early fathers represent a sort of proto-Protestantism, evangelicals will find and should find some wholly unique features of the patristic church that will not be easily squared with their free church perspective. A reader may look in vain to find a teaching or a practice in the early church that offers a precedent for a contemporary religious teaching or practice. The intention of the early church was not to be user-friendly, much less seeker-sensitive,[8] but it does offer the means for transformation if the seeker will seek, knock, and ask. In effect, that is what this book has been about: unraveling the intention and inferences of the tradition so that readers will be better equipped to understand the early church on its own terms.

As a living and dynamic aspect of the Christian faith, the church's tradition is always in the process of development, while providing stability in its canonical aspects. It has functioned as a kind of ongoing conversation that the church has had with itself for over two millennia, enabled by the Holy Spirit. The perennial flexibility and constancy of tradition (or traditioning) enable the church to address contemporary culture with the good news of the gospel. The article produced during Vatican II known as *Dei Verbum* states this progressive dynamic most usefully:

> This tradition which comes from the Apostles develops in the Church with the help of the Holy Spirit. For there is a growth in the understanding of the realities and the words which have been made by believers, who treasure these things in their hearts (see Luke 2:19, 51), through a penetrating understanding of the spiritual realities which they experience. . . . For as the centuries succeed one

8. Robert Wilken observes that in the patristic church's own day various of its aspects were quite different from what the pagans had experienced in Roman culture. The stress on doctrine, the liturgy of the dying and rising God in the flesh, and the resurrection of the dead were for pagans "a wholly different world than they were used to" (Robert Wilken, "Roman Redux," *Christian History* 17, no. 1 [1998]: 44).

another, the Church constantly moves forward toward the fullness of divine truth until the words of God reach their complete fulfillment in her.[9]

Because it is a living entity, the church's tradition articulated over the ages is also subject to reform and renewal—a point on which Roman Catholics and evangelicals generally agree.

In the end, a reception to the ancient tradition enables a believer to determine where the centerpoints of the faith lie and how to distinguish the essential aspects of the faith from the more ephemeral. Making this distinction has always been difficult for Christians and has often been behind the schisms and splits throughout the church's history. But to learn of the fathers and the tradition is to grasp these essentials; it is to become sensitized to the *sensus catholicus*, the sense of what is truly Christian. From this the Christian will greatly benefit in distinguishing what is necessary from what is peripheral or merely trendy.[10] Amid its marvelous diversity, the canonical tradition reveals the consensus and unanimity within the church. Like a row of lamps posted along a winding lane, it continues to illuminate the way of Christian faithfulness for all future pilgrims.

9. *Dei Verbum*, II.8, in *The Documents of Vatican II*, ed. W. Abbott (New York: Association Press, 1966), 116.

10. Boniface Ramsey, *Beginning to Read the Fathers* (Mahwah, N.J.: Paulist Press, 1985), 18.

Patristic Resources in English Translation

Major Collections

Baillie, J., J. McNeill, and H. Van Dussen, eds. *Library of Christian Classics*. Philadelphia: Westminster, 1953–. Selected writings, usually entire, from different ancient authors.

Fathers of the Church. New York: Fathers of the Church, Inc., 1947–. Good quality English translation of select works and helpful introductions.

Harrison, Carol, gen. ed. *The Early Church Fathers*. London: Routledge. Newly translated texts, some for the first time in English, of leading patristic figures: Irenaeus (1997), John Chrysostom (1999), Maximus the Confessor (1996), Ambrose (1997), Origen (1998), Cyril of Jerusalem (2000), Gregory of Nyssa (1999), Cyril of Alexandria (2000), and others forthcoming.

Quasten, J., and J. C. Plumpe, eds. *Ancient Christian Writers*. New York: Newman Press, 1946–. Very good English translations and thorough notes to the text.

Roberts, A., and J. Donaldson, eds. *Ante-Nicene Fathers*. Peabody, Mass.: Hendrickson, 1979. American reprint of the Edinburgh edition, *Ante-Nicene Christian Library* (1864).

Rusch, W., gen ed. *Sources of Early Christian Thought*. Philadelphia: Fortress. Series of whole or large excerpted texts thematically arranged according to theological topic: *The Trinitarian Controversy* (1980); *The Christological Controversy* (1980); *Theological Anthropology* (1981); *Biblical Interpretation in the Early Church* (1984); *Early Christian Spirituality* (1986); *Understandings of the Church* (1986); *The*

Early Church and the State (1982); and *Marriage in the Early Church* (1992).

Schaff, P., and H. Wace, eds. *Nicene and Post-Nicene Fathers of the Christian Church*. First and Second Series. Grand Rapids: Eerdmans, 1983–87. American reprint of the Edinburgh edition. Now reprinted by Hendrickson.

Ward, B., trans. *The Sayings of the Desert Fathers: The Alphabetical Collection*. Kalamazoo, Mich.: Cistercian Publications, 1984.

Excerpted Collections of Texts

Bettenson, H., ed. *The Early Christian Fathers*. Oxford: Oxford University Press, 1967.

———, ed. and trans. *The Later Christian Fathers: A Selection from the Writings of the Fathers from St. Cyril of Jerusalem to St. Leo the Great*. London: Oxford University Press, 1974.

Ehrman, D., ed. *After the New Testament: A Reader in Early Christianity*. New York: Oxford University Press, 1999.

———, and A. Jacobs, eds. *Christianity in Late Antiquity, 300–450 C.E.: A Reader*. New York: Oxford University Press, 2004.

Jurgens, W., ed. and trans. *The Faith of the Early Fathers: A Source Book of Theological and Historical Passages*. Vols. 1–3. Collegeville, Minn.: Liturgical Press, 1970–79.

Pelikan, Jaroslav. *Credo. Historical and Theological Guide to Creeds and Confessions of Faith in the Christian Tradition*. Vols. 1–4. New Haven: Yale University Press, 2003.

Stevenson, J., ed. *Creeds, Councils, and Controversies: Documents Illustrating the History of the Church AD 337–461.* London: SPCK, 1989.

———. *A New Eusebius: Documents Illustrating the History of the Church to AD 337.* London: SPCK, 1987.

Wiles, M. F., and M. Santer. *Documents in Early Christian Thought.* New York: Cambridge University Press, 1975.

Research Tools

Berardino, A. di, ed. *Patrology.* Vol. 4. Westminster, Md.: Christian Classics, 1988.

———, and B. Studer, eds. *History of Theology: The Patristic Period.* Collegeville, Minn.: Liturgical Press, 1997.

Chadwick, H., and E. Evans. *Atlas of the Christian Church.* New York: Facts on File Publications, 1987.

Ferguson, E., ed. *Encyclopedia of Early Christianity.* 2nd ed. New York: Garland Publishers, 1993.

Hultgren, A., and S. Haggmark, eds. *The Earliest Christian Heretics: Readings from Their Opponents.* Minneapolis: Fortress, 1996.

Kelly, J. N. D. *Early Christian Creeds.* 3rd ed. London: Longman, 1972.

———. *Early Christian Doctrines.* London: A. C. Black, 1977.

Pelikan, J. *The Christian Tradition: A History of the Development of Doctrine.* Vol. 1, *The Emergence of the Catholic Tradition (100–600).* Chicago: University of Chicago Press, 1971.

Quasten, J., ed. *Patrology.* Vols. 1–3. Westminster, Md.: Christian Classics, 1983.

Ramsey, Boniface. *Beginning to Read the Fathers.* Mahwah, N.J.: Paulist Press, 1985.

van der Meer, F., and C. Mohrmann, eds. *Atlas of the Early Christian World.* London: Nelson, 1958.

Walford, A., trans. *Encyclopedia of the Early Church.* Vols. 1–2. New York: Oxford University Press, 1992.

Websites for Patristic Studies

Augustine of Hippo: http://ccat.sas.upenn.edu/jod/augustine. This is a site maintained by J. J. O'Donnell dedicated to the study of Augustine. It offers many texts of Augustine's works as well as many aids related to the study of Augustine's life, works, and influence.

Christian Classics Ethereal Library (CCEL): http://www.ccel.org. The CCEL is an electronic library of Christian resources from a variety of time periods and traditions. It makes available numerous texts and research tools.

Early Church Fathers (CCEL): http://www.ccel.org/fathers2. The Early Church Fathers is a digitized format of the *Ante-Nicene Fathers (ANF)*, Nicene and Post-Nicene Fathers Series 1 (NPNF1), and Nicene and Post-Nicene Fathers Series 2 (NPNF2).

The Ecole Initiative: http://www2.evansville.edu/ecoleweb. This is an extensive hypertext encyclopedia of early church history. Many of its links to the actual writings of the early church period are links to the previously mentioned CCEL website. However, it offers added features such as glossary essays and articles on numerous topics, many links to Christian art, and helpful tools relating to chronology and geography.

ICLnet Guide to Early Church Documents: http://www.iclnet.org/pub/resources/christian-history.html. This hypertext document contains pointers to Internet-accessible files relating to the early church, including canonical documents, creeds, the writings of the apostolic fathers, and other historical texts relevant to church history.

Rich Tatum's glossary of church history: http://tatumweb.com/churchrodent. This glossary provides brief definitions and descriptions of terms, people, and places important to the history of Christianity from its inception to the modern period.

Index